SHATTERING THE SILENCE

SHATTERING THE SILENCE

Telling the Church
the Truth About
Kids and Sexuality

DAVID LEWIS
CARLEY DODD
DARRYL TIPPENS

Christian Communications
P. O. Box 150
Nashville, TN 37202

DEDICATION

We dedicate this book to our teens whose bright future in God's kingdom gives us immense hope.

ACKNOWLEDGMENTS

We deeply appreciate the outstanding manuscript and data preparation staff for this book and for their significant contribution to this project: Roberta Brown, Anna Cloud, Chris Heard, B.J. McMichael, David Cheatham and Elaine Reynolds.

Special appreciation goes to Dr. Ian Fair, dean of the College of Biblical Studies, Abilene Christian University, for his support of the research for this project. His dynamic leadership and commitment to practical ministry gave us the dream.

We thank the many youth ministers who supported this project. Without their efforts, this project never would have become a reality.

David wishes to thank Pam, Israel, Jeremy and Christopher for hanging in there with yet another project, in hopes that after this one Dad would come home.

Carley wishes to thank Ada, Jeremy, Matthew, Philip and Jennifer for the family time they sacrificed, while offering incredible emotional and spiritual support. You gave the gift of yourselves, which is more than any man can ask. For no greater love has been shown.

Darryl wishes to acknowledge the special contribution of Anne, Kyle and Jeff, who not only taught him most of what he knows about good parenting but also who taught him the deep truth that home is where his best friends are.

CONTENTS

CHAPTER
1

A TIME TO SPEAK

"There is a time for everything, and a season for every activity under heaven . . . a time to be silent and a time to speak" (Ecclesiastes 3:1,7).

" 'I tell you,' he replied, 'if they keep quiet, the stones will cry out' " (Luke 19:40).

"It is written: 'I believed; therefore I have spoken.' With that same spirit of faith we also believe and therefore speak" (2 Corinthians 4:13).

Melanie was in trouble. Eighteen, away from home for the first time and feeling very much alone, she found herself sexually involved with a young man she hardly knew. After a few months, this attractive daughter of God-fearing, churchgoing parents was distraught, more alone than ever—and pregnant. Yet she could hardly turn to her family for support or help. After all, her father was an important leader in his congregation. Melanie simply could not face the shame that would come with having a baby. Finally, she decided upon her "solution." With funds

1

borrowed from a roommate, she would have an abortion.

A few days later Melanie drove to an abortion clinic in a nearby town, a safe distance from family, church and friends. She was all alone in her trial, or so she thought. As she checked in at the desk, Melanie was greeted with the nurse's sardonic remark: "We just performed abortions on four other girls from your town. Honey, you girls should have car-pooled."

"Honey, you girls should have car-pooled." Those stinging words contained a point that the nurse may not have intended. Since those terrible days, Melanie has bravely sought to work through her griefs, her wrong turns, and her mistakes. But she cannot forget, nor can we, the point behind the nurse's derisive words, which is that the kids from respectable homes and religious communities may be in as much trouble as anyone else and that everyone, church kids included, is a part of America's sexual revolution.

Are Christian values being eroded completely in our day? How many other Melanies are out there? Is her story at all typical?

The Poverty of Data

The fact is, until very recently we simply could not answer such questions intelligently or accurately. Until now, even if Christians were willing to face such questions (and many were not), answers were sketchy, ill-informed, and often skewed by accidents of personal experience, conventional wisdom, random anecdotes, myth and prejudice.

Because ample evidence shows that some teens, like Melanie, have been caught up in the sexual revolution, some pessimists have concluded hastily that a whole generation of Christian young people have succumbed to the new immorality. Some ministers have told us, "Eighty percent of the kids in my congregation are having sex." Others have said in despair, "No one believes in virginity anymore."

But are these pessimistic assessments correct? Are the church's young people undergoing the same moral changes as the dominant secular society in which they dwell? Where significant shifts in behavior are occurring, who is to blame? What can be done to remedy the negative shifts? How do families and local churches figure in the changes? What can they do to strengthen the ethical lives of our young? "Good questions," we think, but few seem to have substantial, documented answers.

The Genesis of This Project

We have searched for answers to these questions for several reasons. We have met several Melanies (and Ryans and Marks too), children from the community of faith who are struggling with desperately complex and, at times, almost overwhelming problems. They are our children, the youth of the body of Christ, with whom and for whom we have felt much anguish. As teachers, ministers and therapists, we have seen the need for information and understanding. For too long we have operated in the dark about what is happening to our youth. The time has come to move from ignorance to knowledge and from fear to understanding, for without correct information, we are frustrated and handicapped guides.

Without real understanding, we may even be dangerous guides to our children, despite our sincerest intentions. We may actually cause their deaths, quite literally. Today, accurate information about sexuality is no longer optional because it may determine the physical and spiritual survival of our children. Sometimes not knowing the truth is more dangerous and costly than knowing. In an age of many sexually transmitted diseases, including AIDS, there is a new urgency to talk openly and to talk straight.

Parents and church leaders who think they can best protect their teens by wrapping sex in a veil of silence will pay a terrible price sooner or later. Unwillingness to talk frankly and precisely may prove fatal. We know that many of today's teens are sexually active. A recent unofficial survey in one high school revealed that one out of 100 students carries the AIDS virus. National testing shows that one out of every 500 college students carries the AIDS virus.[1]

In such environments where sexual freedom is considered acceptable and myths about "safe sex" are commonplace, do we have a responsibility to shatter the silence? To fail to speak frankly and openly to our teens and to one another goes beyond irresponsibility. It approaches criminality.

Dr. Sol Gordon is an eminent authority on teenagers' behavior in America today. Although he does not speak as a Christian believer, he has a vital message for church leaders and parents. Recently he addressed a conference of youth ministers in Atlanta:

I really don't know much about churches of Christ and I hardly know anything at all about youth ministry, but one thing I know about organized religion as a whole is we are doing nothing to stem the tide of rising sexuality. Last year 500 kids lost their lives because they believed a lie that masturbation with a noose around their necks was the ultimate orgasm. They believed that lie because no one told them the truth, especially you church people. As the papal decision is announced because smoke rises from the chimney, so in the same way, there is no smoke rising from churches, synagogues, cathedrals anymore, announcing the direct message about sexual problems to our young people, and you have further failed to offer any coping strategies.[2]

Gordon went on to say, with tears in his eyes, that organized religion as a whole has failed its young.

Is Gordon's assessment too extreme, too bleak? We may wish to think so, but abundant evidence supports his charges. We believe that young people are going to die, both physically and spiritually, unless we look carefully at the subject of teen-age sexuality and tell what we see.

Although some persons may feel uncomfortable thinking about the following information, we believe the truth about this subject is vitally important to effective ministry. "You will know the truth, and the truth will set you free," Jesus tells us (John 8:32). This biblical concept has a valid application here. Until we know precisely the terrain of the world in which our adolescents struggle daily, how can we hope to minister to them properly? Without accurate understanding—truth—there can be no genuine liberation, psychological or spiritual. Proper loving presupposes a measure of knowledge and understanding. Compassion and guidance, however well meant, are ineffectual and misguided when uninformed by genuine understanding.

A great deal of scientific data will be presented in the following pages. The data were gathered from a carefully constructed survey instrument administered to 2,300 young people scientifically selected from all regions of the United States. In an unprecedented way, we have attempted to render an accurate portrait of the church's young people. We make every effort to base our conclusions on carefully gathered research.[3]

Even so, our scientific approach should never obscure our personal concerns or the personal dimensions of this work. As struggling parents of struggling teen-agers ourselves, we have a deeply personal interest in the outcome of this story. No family is immune to the potent forces reshaping our society, certainly not ours. We hope to show through this book that firm knowledge can lead to compassionate ministry to our young. Above all, we hope that parents and church leaders will be led to informed action and compassionate caring, not futile hand-wringing.

In this matter, as in others, we are called to be "wise as serpents." If we are, the facts about our young people's sexuality, beliefs, concerns and lifestyles can become the foundation for better parenting and ministry. We hope this chapter, which previews some of our major findings, will serve to stir Christian parents and church leaders to learn more, so they can give better care to those in their charge. More than ever, our children need our loving guidance, our wisdom and our prayerful concern.

An Overview

Having spent years polling, interviewing and counseling young people, we have extensive personal and scientific data to answer an array of critical questions about our young people—what they believe, what they practice, and how they cope in a sexual society increasingly hostile to Christian values. We not only have learned a great deal about specific adolescent *behaviors* (such as sexual activity, pornography usage and incest) and *attitudes* (toward church, family, friends and self), but we also have learned a great deal about the *environmental* factors that tend to encourage or discourage such behavior. Sexual attitudes and behaviors, our research confirms, are intimately linked to the particular environment in which each adolescent dwells. Family life, congregational styles, friendships and the media, it will become apparent, powerfully shape a young person's resolve either to break the biblical moral code or to live within its limits.

In this chapter, we provide a synopsis, a composite portrait, of the thinking and sexual behavior of teenagers who attend churches of Christ. We summarize the data concerning such matters as virginity, promiscuity and pornography. Following the summary of attitudes and behavior, we describe some of the major environmental factors (such as home, family and media) that can dramatically impinge upon adolescent sexuality. Understanding these environmental influences is especially important because they are something over which adults have some control.

Finally, we begin the necessary process of pointing toward solutions. Recommendations will be treated more fully in later chapters, but from the beginning we must see that there are escape routes from the morass.

SEXUAL ATTITUDES AND BEHAVIOR: A SYNOPSIS

Virginity

Sexual activity is common among today's American teen-agers; however, Christian teen-agers fare better than the typical adolescent. The virginity rate among non-religious American teens stands at 40 percent according to some researchers, but our survey reveals a 71.5 percent virginity rate. Our research reveals that virginity rates decline, as one could expect, with age. Twelve-year-olds have a virginity rate of 93 percent, while 20-year-olds have a 56 percent rate.

Considering national norms of 40 percent, the 71.5 percent average is surprisingly high, yet our figure is reasonably consistent with trends uncovered by other surveys of religious young people. Josh McDowell studied 1,400 young people in a survey sponsored by eight evangelical churches. By age 18, 43 percent of McDowell's sample had had sexual intercourse; that is to say, he found a 57 percent virginity rate.

How promiscuous are our adolescents? Of the non-virgin group (28.5 percent), almost one half vowed to abstain from sexual activity in the future; another 40 percent intended to have intercourse only in "a committed relationship"; and 10 percent intended to be active sexually outside of a committed relationship. It appears that the first half of this group of non-virgins has learned something from past mistakes. The other half seems to fall into two problem groups: The 40 percent who are involved in sexual relationships in a quest for illusory promises of security and acceptance, and the 10 percent who claim no interest in biblical morality.

When we asked the non-virgins with whom they had sexual relations, the respondents described a wide range of relationships, but one fact stands out with singular clarity: *90 percent of the non-virgins were in a steady dating relationship when the sexual experience occurred.* This fact challenges each parent and minister to provide biblical resources to help teens cope with the weighty demands of steady dating. Recently a concerned family physician counseled a young patient about her sexual behavior. The woman replied, "What am I supposed to do? How am I to deal with my feelings? The church has never helped me to deal with passion." The sentiment no doubt echoes the feelings of many thousands of teens today.

Technical Virginity/Intimate Touching

The news on virginity is encouraging. However, the research also reveals how frequently teens resort to physical touch as a substitute for sexual intercourse. We call this touching "technical virginity" or "intimate touching." Throughout this book we use these terms to mean the fondling of breasts and genitals, including mutual masturbation. The technical virgin thinks, "Anything goes, short of penetration."

Three-fourths of the adolescents in our survey admit to intimate touching. Specifically, 15 percent resort to it regularly, and 60 percent have practiced it some. Only 25 percent have never practiced it. Although one may be pleased with a fairly high rate of virginity among religious adolescents, this success is severely tempered by the widespread practice of intimate touching.

The way some teen-agers view technical virginity is evident in Amy's story. At a church party the kids paired off, and Amy and a boy went to a back room where they fondled to the point of orgasm. When the youth minister discovered their actions and confronted them, Amy responded, "Well, what else can we do? We can't have sex, you know." In addition to betraying a distorted sense of purity, Amy's justification also points to a failure in our teaching. Have we emphasized virginity in a manner that obscures the biblical call to chaste behavior in its fullest sense? The practice of technical virginity suggests that our teaching on sexual purity may be poorly understood, if not flawed. Many of our young people are first-class scribes and Pharisees when it comes to sexual purity; they are able to strain at gnats and swallow camels. Clearly, we must re-examine how we teach moral purity.

Pregnancy, Abortion and STD

We asked several questions about pregnancy, abortion, sexually transmitted diseases (STD), and other related topics. Two percent of our sample indicated they had been pregnant, compared with approximately 10 percent for the general teen-age population in the United States.

Only 1.1 percent of the students in our survey have had an abortion, a figure that compares favorably to the 4 percent rate for Protestant college students, revealed in a recent Gallup poll. This rather low figure, one must note, is partly the result of the lower level of sexual activity of religious teens, which in turn means a lower pregnancy rate. For those religious females who have been sexually active, the abortion rate is, of course, higher.

Very few respondents give general approval to abortion: 55 percent view it as morally questionable, although justified in cases of rape and certain dangerous conditions for the mother; 35 percent see abortion as murder; 6 percent see it as a reasonable solution to pregnancy when marriage was not realistic; 3 percent approve it as a "convenience"; and 1.5 percent perceive abortion as an important means of population control.

Despite the epidemic nature of a variety of sexually transmitted diseases today, the vast majority of people in the sample have never contracted a sexually transmitted disease (98 percent). Of those who have (just under 2 percent), the types of illness were as follows: genital herpes (22 percent), syphilis (18 percent), gonorrhea (11 percent), and AIDS (7.4 percent). The remainder of those who had suffered from STD stated they had some other type of sexually transmitted disease, but it was unreported or unknown at the time of this survey.

Incidence of Incest

Even the most competent family therapists report difficulty in measuring the occurrence of incest. In psychiatric hospitals, obviously a clinical population, over 60 percent of the patients have been sexually abused at one time or another. This seems to be a consistent finding across the nation, at least in terms of the clinical population.

But what about the general population, and what about the churchgoing population? Dr. Ed Coates and Dr. Gayle Napier, two respected marriage and family therapists, believe that up to 40 percent of females within conservative and fundamentalist churches have been sexually abused during their formative years.

In our survey 94 percent report no experience with incest. Of the 6 percent who have been victims, about one-fourth of the cases involved the father; an additional 14 percent involve the stepfather; 5 percent the mother, and 1 percent the stepmother. The category labelled "other" was the most frequently checked.

This figure of 6 percent may seem low; however, the problem is greater when one considers that incestuous behavior often is unreported because victims tend to repress and deny their traumatizing experiences. Therapists report that some patients can recall the experience only under hypnosis or after intensive therapy. In any case, we are talking about a substantial number of victims.

Pornography, Drugs and Alcohol

Our society is fairly awash in a sea of sexually explicit materials in the form of sleazy magazines, "trash TV," and pornographic films easily available in neighborhood video shops. How is this deluge of pornographic material affecting our youth? We asked our respondents how frequently they looked at sexually explicit materials, such as *Playboy, Penthouse, Playgirl* and X-rated videos. In summary, 46 percent of our teen-agers have had some exposure to these forms of pornography, but 54 percent reported never being exposed to sexually explicit material.

Like pornography, alcohol and drugs have become a universal concern in American society. Consequently, our study examined substance abuse to see how it may contribute to sexual immorality. We asked the degree to which each respondent had used drugs or alcohol in order to enhance sexual experience. Twelve percent reported that they had used drugs or alcohol in this way. Of this 12 percent, 94 percent had used alcohol to enhance their sexual experience, while 41 percent had used marijuana, 14 percent ecstasy, 12 percent cocaine, and 11 percent some other drug. Clearly, Christian teens are not immune to the substance abuse that has become so pronounced in our culture.

Homosexuality

Given a culture where homosexual behavior is encouraged in some quarters and even flaunted in others, one naturally wonders if adolescents in the church feel either neutral or ambivalent toward homosexuality. The fact is that 90 percent of the adolescents believe that homosexual behavior is morally wrong. Nine percent say that it "depends on the situation." Less than 1 percent indicate that it is not a sin at all.

Our sample reveals a generally conservative consensus concerning how homosexuals should be treated. Of the repondents, 62 percent said we should accept homosexuals if they are penitent and change their behavior; 21 percent said we should accept them in church "no matter what"; 14 percent said we should exclude them because of their homosexuality "no matter what"; and 3 percent said we should accept them if they are "penitent" but continue their homosexual practices. Most young people believe that homosexual practices are immoral, although many accept homosexual persons on some basis (if they are penitent and live chaste lives, for example).

Self-Perception and Sexuality

Teens, like adults, are very much affected by their perceptions. How they see themselves and their world has much to do with how they behave. We asked a variety of questions to determine how teens view their peers and themselves. Do they like themselves? Do they believe they control their own lives? Do they feel loved, worthy, competent?

The answers to such questions are important and revealing as subsequent chapters will show. Generally, a high regard for self is closely linked to moral behavior. Those who feel competent, satisfied with life, and valuable have greater stores of resistance to temptation and greater motivation to maintain their purity. On the other hand, adolescents who feel hopeless, powerless or fatalistic about life have much less ability to resist sexual temptation. They see themselves as victims, and their self-deprecating thoughts prove to be prophetic. They become sexually involved precisely because they feel so fatalistic and powerless. With such a mindset, being laughed at or rejected by one's buddies becomes unbearable. These teen-agers must bow to the pressures of others, doing whatever others want them to at the moment, whatever the cost.

Parents, teachers and ministers have a great deal of responsibility to teach students self-worth, which is based upon God's estimate of them, and significance, which is founded upon their divine origin and Christ's saving work. Our survey underscores the necessity of teaching the sacred value of every human being: "For God did not give us a spirit of timidity, but a spirit of power, of love and of self-discipline" (2 Timothy 1:7).

Our findings dramatize the universal need to be loved by others and to feel God's love. The love that teen-agers seek is the love that every human desperately needs—a steadfast love that endures forever. Our teens must feel loved by others, and they must return that love in a proper way. Perhaps the central task of youth and family ministry today is to assure children that they are loved completely by God. The Father loves them with "an everlasting love" (Jeremiah 31:3).

But how do they experience this great truth as something more than an intellectual principle? How do we help them feel in their hearts and souls God's yearning for them? The answers should be of concern to every Christian parent and church leader.

THE TEEN'S ENVIRONMENT: CHURCH, FAMILY, MEDIA AND FRIENDS

Sexual ethics do not mature in a vacuum, nor do fully formed sexual attitudes spring forth magically at puberty. Rather, sexual beliefs are slowly shaped and nurtured in a particular cultural environment. The local congregation, family life, the media and friendships can greatly impact the thinking and behavior of our teens. Subsequent chapters explain in detail how these various factors affect teen-agers' lives. Parents and church leaders will want to pay special attention to these factors because even small changes in the environment can encourage healthy improvements.

Congregational Styles

Does the church really affect the behavior of its youth? Does Brother Davis' Sunday morning lesson have any perceptible bearing on what Susan and Derek do with each other Saturday night? Do the flurry of youth meetings, "lock-ins," prayer sessions, and summer mission trips directed by energetic and well-meaning youth ministers have much to do with how our teen-agers practice their sexuality? In general, there is good news here. For example, virginity rates are much higher among teen-agers who frequently attend worship and Bible study. In fact, an active, vibrant church experience definitely encourages a higher moral life, though of course church involvement cannot guarantee high morals.

Unfortunately, not all communities of faith are equally supportive of young people, our research shows. In some churches a prevailing mood of rigidity and legalism actually deters moral growth. Other congregations do an excellent job of fostering personal faith in teen-agers. Not surprisingly, those teens who own their faith personally are much more likely to live morally pure lives. Thoughtful church leaders will want to assess their own fellowship to see if the "congregational style" is truly contributing to the sexual maturity of their adolescents.

Family Life

From what sort of families do our young people come? How much do parents influence their teen's moral choices? How much do adolescents "buy into" their parents' belief system? Does parental advice count for much as the teen-ager enters the sexual jungle? Mothers and fathers often question their worth as their influence fades, just as external influences loom ever more powerful in their children's lives.

Yet good news can be given despite our worst fears. Our youth say that their parents are influential. An encouraging 88 percent said their parents were "somewhat" or "very" influential on their sexual attitudes and beliefs. Almost all of the respondents see themselves as influenced by parents; a healthy 92 percent express some level of identification with their parents' values.

When parental instruction seems muted by outside voices and when parents feel pushed aside as their teens take stage center, parents will find it worth recalling that in most cases the teaching from childhood leaves an indelible mark.

Media Influences

When one considers that more Americans own televisions than have refrigerators or indoor plumbing and that TV watching ranks as the third most important activity of life in terms of hours devoted to it (second only to sleep and work), one has to consider the role of the media in the lives of our young people. In light of the pervasiveness of the media, including music and movies (which are especially formidable influences in teen-agers' lives), it becomes especially important to measure the impact of the media. Forty-six percent of those surveyed say that the media have had a major impact on their thinking about sex. Teens tell us that explicit love scenes in soap operas, racy song lyrics, and suggestive scenes in movies are major sources of sexual influence. Only 24 percent claim that the media have little or no impact on their sexuality.

Friends and Faith

Our research confirms in several ways the basic truth that healthy friendships encourage ethical living. On the other hand, when children identify closely with troubled and rebellious peers, difficulties are almost certain. Fortunately, most of our teen-agers draw their close friends from the church set. Almost 90 percent of our respondents make religious peers their primary friends. Because such friendships tend to encourage spiritual growth and long-term church involvement, healthy youth and family programs will make the formation of positive peer networks a primary goal.

Concluding Concerns

When one compares the kind of data we find in this survey with other national surveys of teens in the United States, one can see clearly that religiosity and churchgoing do have a considerable effect on attitudes and ethical behavior. For the most part, our church kids are virgin, opposed to permissiveness and abortion, and in harmony with parental values.

However, we have reason for concern. We are genuinely concerned for the 6 percent (or more) of our youths who are victims of incest. We are concerned for the adolescents who report using alcohol and drugs as a way of enhancing sexual experiences. Use of chemicals in this way indicates a lack of coping skills and may reflect the degree to which our youth have entered the culture of narcissism in which pleasure is their god.

In addition, we must note the unfortunate inference that as a religious group we may have excelled in the letter of the law, as reported by high rates of virginity, but have failed in the spirit of the law, illustrated by the prevalance of technical virginity. A large number of our teens are resorting to various forms of intimate touching, including mutual masturbation, but are considering themselves to be "chaste" because they do not "go all the way."

Too many of our adolescents do not grasp the meaning of biblical love or the Lordship of Christ. They scarcely understand the Christian ideal of consecration. To tell them not to have sex will do little good. To teach them how to be sexual beings, informed by genuine faith, is our task.

Finally, we must note that many of our young people turn to sex because they don't know where else to turn to cure their loneliness or their longing for affection. They are deluded, yes, like many of their parents. But their wrong turns indicate something momentous: namely, their restless, God-ordained search for love and acceptance. Although adults may be powerless to control the worst features of a hedonistic culture saturated with sexual messages, they can still do much to minister to their children's emotional and spiritual longings, thereby diminishing the lure of the sexual "quick fix." Lewis Smedes tells us in *Sex for Christians*:

> We are all hungry for closeness. Young people feel the need most urgently. They grew up in neighborhoods of indifference; they have often felt alienated from their parents' styles and values; and they are lonely within the huge information factories called universities. Besides, they have become skeptical about the institutional side of life in general—of marriage in particular. So why not find closeness in the simplest way . . . ?"[4]

The deep roots of loneliness often feed the wrong kind of behavior; yet, fortunately, if we see the nature of the problem, we can provide real help to our young. At the very least, we can be at home and present to them, both physically and emotionally.

In *Seeds of Hope*, Henri Nouwen shrewdly observes: "One way to express the spiritual crisis of our time is to say that most of us have an address but cannot be found there."[5] This observation literally describes the suburban streets where many of us live, but the observation also is a tragically accurate description of many families. The arrow of responsibility seems to be pointing in the direction of parents and church leaders. The cure for our children's sexual problems may require a dose of medicine on our part.

Are we ready to face our teens and their place in the world of human sexuality? Can we face each other on this subject? Can we face ourselves? We hope so.

We hope this chapter is the beginning of a necessary journey toward a truthful and honest view of our church, our teens and ourselves in the area of human sexuality. Our integrity as the people of God requires that we make this journey to awareness, however unpleasant it may be. There is a time for everything, and a season for every activity under heaven. Now is the time to shatter the silence.

Endnotes

1. David Neff, "Will Your Child Get AIDS?" *Christianity Today* 22 September 1989: 15.
2. Sol Gordon. Lecture. Conference on Adolescents and their Families. Atlanta, GA, April 1985.
3. These data were gathered from students at five Christian universities and from teen-agers in congregations of churches of Christ representing all regions of the United States. The sample is regionally weighted according to the distribution of churches of Christ in the United States. The margin

of error for this sample of 2,300 respondents, at a 95 percent confidence level, is ± 2 percent.

Because this study is intended for a lay audience, we have avoided excessive detail about our research methods. However, one should note that our study was conducted according to the limits of appropriate social survey methods.

Some readers may raise questions about our freedom to draw conclusions based upon correlations. It is true that simple correlations do not prove causation. Causal links are, strictly speaking, difficult to prove. Nonetheless, for two important reasons, from a scientific point of view, we are able to infer causation in this study. First, when there is a reason to draw a conclusion based upon established theory, then it should come as no surprise when we find a correlation that supports the established theory. In many cases, the correlation established in our research eloquently supports such established *a priori* theories. Second, when other extraneous variables are controlled using multiple correlational techniques, researchers can then remove the effects of other potentially causal variables, thus inviting one to make causal inferences. In other words, when a host of variables is examined by the use of multiple regression and path analysis, then predictive inferences are reasonable, if not compelling. For further details, see the epilogue and Appendix I on pages 160 and 164.

4. Lewis B. Smedes, *Sex for Christians* (Grand Rapids: Eerdmans, 1976), 139.

5. Henri Nouwen, *Seeds of Hope*, ed. Robert Durback (New York: Bantam Books, 1989), 12.

CHAPTER
2

SEEING THEMSELVES, SEEING THE WORLD: SELF-PERCEPTION AND SEXUALITY

"Though seeing, they do not see; though hearing, they do not hear or understand" (Matthew 13:13).

"For God did not give us a spirit of timidity, but a spirit of power, of love and of self-discipline" (2 Timothy 1:7).

" 'Launch into the deep,' says Jacques Ellul, 'and you shall see.' The secret of seeing is, then, the pearl of great price."—Annie Dillard, Pilgrim at Tinker Creek.

In the academy-award-winning film *Lawrence of Arabia*, two views of the world clash in a dramatic way. T.E. Lawrence, the legendary British officer serving in the Middle East during World War I, decides to lead 50 Arabs across a treacherous desert, one so scorchingly hot that it is called the "Devil's Anvil." By crossing at night, however, Lawrence and his comrades succeed. But, just as the sun begins to rise and just as they reach the desert's edge, they

22

discover that during the night one of the men has fallen from his camel and has been left behind.

Most of the Arabs want to push on, for to turn back means certain death on the Devil's Anvil. They want to push on also because they see the world in a certain way. They are true fatalists. The man lost in the desert was fated to die, they believe. "It is written that he should die. Let us go on," they tell Lawrence. But Lawrence views reality quite differently. His universe is much more open-ended. The script of life has not yet been written. With compelling intensity, the British soldier shouts, "It is *not* written that he shall die!" Lawrence turns back alone, and to everyone's amazement he rides into the searing desert to retrieve the lost man, which he does.

Robert Bolt's screenplay of *Lawrence of Arabia* describes two sharply contrasting views of life, two different ways of seeing, and each leads to a particular form of action (or inaction). In modern times, poets, philosophers and pyschologists have been fascinated with human perception. How does our view of reality affect what we see and how we act? What factors determine what we are able to see? In fact, many things shape one's perceptions — language, experience, cultural patterns, religious beliefs, education and emotions. All these things color our thinking and affect our actions.

When we consider parents and children, we also realize that differing capacities of perception are involved. Emotional maturity, attitudes and experience condition what we are capable of seeing, how we feel about ourselves, and how able we are to cope with temptation and stress. Some adolescents are like the Arabs in *Lawrence of Arabia*. For them, "all of life is written already." This fatalistic outlook, this conviction that they have little or no control over the events in their lives, makes them quite vulnerable to sexual temptation. On the other hand, some adolescents believe they do have a measure of control over their lives. Choices should be made, and they can make them. These youths see themselves as agents, not victims. From their points of view, their life stories have not yet been scripted. Significantly, these youths have much more resolve to direct their own lives and resist sexual temptation.

So, we understand that perceptions affect behavior in powerful ways. "Be careful how you look at the world; it's like that," Professor Erich Heller has said. The point behind the professor's exaggeration is that we must be careful how we see the world, for surely it will *seem* as though that is actually the way the world is. We must examine our understandings of the world, for they vastly affect how we respond to life.

This being so, our research led us to ask a few key questions about how our teens perceive themselves and their world. In particular, we asked questions about self-perceptions. Do teens view themselves as persons of value and worthy of love? In general, do they consider themselves as competent? We also asked questions to determine whether they believe they have a measure of control over their lives. Is the "locus" of control within themselves or outside themselves? Do they have a measure of control, or has their life story already been scripted? The answers to such questions prove to have momentous consequences.

Self-Concept, Virginity and Pornography

We asked our respondents a number of questions about their self-image. As one might expect, youths with positive views of self are more likely to be virgins. Teens who feel competent, capable of doing things well, satisfied with life, and valuable have greater motivation to preserve their chastity.

- Those who see themselves as doing well (being competent) have a 73 percent virginity rate; those who don't feel competent have a 67 percent rate.
- Those who report often feeling happy (life satisfaction) have a 76 percent virginity rate compared with those who report feeling unhappy, who have a 58 percent virginity rate.
- Those who feel useful (valuable) have a 70 percent virginity rate; those who often feel useless have a 64 percent virginity rate.

We also looked at self-esteem and its correlation with pornography usage. As with virginity rates, self-esteem correlates positively to the avoidance of pornography.

- Those who feel useful have a 56 percent rate of avoiding pornography, while those who feel useless have a 41 percent rate.
- Those who report feeling inner happiness have a 61 percent rate of avoiding pornography compared to 46 percent who are not happy.

In view of these findings, Christian parents and church leaders ought to reconsider their mission to "train a child in the way he should go." Traditionally, this has meant either to ground the child in the doctrines of the faith or to teach and enforce certain ethical rules. But our mission is really much larger. If we do not give our children a biblical world view and also a concept of self that is wholesome and affirming, our research strongly suggests that our children will find it quite difficult to accept and practice the teachings of Scripture. Paul teaches us never to drive our children to resentment or discouragement, but to correct and guide them (Ephesians 6:4). Surely guidance in the fullest sense means teaching a wholesome, positive view of the world.

The pattern is clear: Self-esteem contributes to positive behavior. Our adolescents tend to live up to or down to the image they hold of themselves. Certainly, this is reason enough to instill in our youths a strong sense of their dignity and value before God as bearers of the divine image.

Self-Esteem and Family Values

Self-esteem not only seems to encourage sexual morality, but it also seems to encourage the acceptance of positive family values in general. Adolescents who feel good about themselves are much more likely to adopt their parents' value system, at the highest level.

- 23 percent of those who perceive themselves to be highly competent identify strongly with parental values compared with 11 percent of those who have a low opinion of their competency.
- 24 percent of those who see themselves as valuable identify with parental values at the highest level, but among those who devalue themselves, only 9 percent do so.
- 24 percent of those who see themselves as useful accept parental values, while 13 percent of those who feel useless accept parental values.
- 40 percent of those who express personal contentment accept parental influence compared with

18 percent of those who wish they were someone
else.

When self-esteem is not conferred upon a child
and when parents fail to bless their children with a
profound sense of worth, lasting harm, which tran-
scends generations, can occur. This point is well
illustrated in the case of Richard, an elder in the
church who suffered from a poor relationship with
his father. During Richard's adolescent years his father ignored him and made him feel utterly worthless.
So Richard grew up with a terrible view of himself.
Although he eventually became a successful business-
man, a respected family man, and a strong leader in
his church, Richard continued to have severe doubts
about himself. He also fumbled in his role as the
father of a daughter also needing loving attention.

After his father died, Richard invested a great deal
of time in his first-born son, Rick Jr. Richard lavished
attention on his son, and the boy developed a positive
regard for his dad and for himself. However, despite
Richard's efforts not to repeat his father's mistakes,
despite all the time he spent with his son, he still
failed part of his family. He completely neglected his
daughter, Kellie. Perhaps the neglect was uninten-
tional. Just the same, Kellie felt rejected and worthless.

When we talked to her, she explained it like this:
"My dad was always doing church work and spending
time with my brother. I never was quite sure that he
really loved me. In any case, I never felt like I could
do anything worthwhile, and I sure didn't feel very
secure about myself."

In his anxious attempt to restore a lost relationship
with his own father vicariously through his son,
Richard still repeated his father's error by neglecting

27

his second child. The consequences were severe. What Kellie could not find in her father, she found in the arms of another man. She became pregnant at 17.

Heather was 14 when she was referred to a family therapist. Heather's father was acting in a positive, proper way toward her, trying to increase her self-esteem by showing her respect, attention and fatherly affection. However, her mother was so insecure that she became jealous of Heather's relationship with the father. Rather than honestly face her own insecurity, the mom began to demean and humiliate Heather. The mother's attempt to drive a wedge between the father and daughter deeply wounded the girl. Heather became bulimic, and she also became sexually active.

Both Heather and Kellie illustrate a common phenomenon among adolescents: Poor self-esteem is fertile ground for promiscuous behavior.

Heather and Kellie are typical of adolescents who are vulnerable because their self-images are so frail. How do we identify such damaged young people? What would their profile look like? Parents, teachers and others who work with adolescents should note the following characteristics:

- *Lack of motivation*—often evident with failing grades and a desire to drop out of school.
- *Increased frustration*—unresolved anger is rooted in feelings of personal inadequacy and often this devaluation of self shows up in numerous acting-out behaviors, such as lying, theft, verbal and physical abusiveness, and other destructive behavior.
- *Unsuitable friends*—low self-esteem leads to problem friendships; youth with low self-esteem search out friends who assure immediate acceptance and approval.

- *Frequent conflicts*—these teens are usually unwilling to resolve conflict with family and peers and typically lack the ability to be assertive, especially when parents are excessively controlling.
- *Anxiety and depression*—if a teen sees herself as hopeless, helpless or incompetent, that perception easily leads to anxiety, which, if unchecked, grows into depression.

Freedom vs. Fatalism

Hopelessness, the sense of not being in control of one's life, often characterizes the life of the promiscuous teen-ager. When Laurie was 6, she was sexually abused by her older brother. The abuse went on for three years before she felt safe to tell her mother. When Laurie finally did tell, the mother could not acknowledge the painful truth; she accused Laurie of lying.

Now, nine years later, Laurie reports to her youth minister that she is sexually active and has been since she was 13 with more partners than she can remember. She feels guilt over two abortions, and she feels absolutely powerless to control her life. Every time she goes out with a boy, she finds it impossible to say no. And now she pleads with the youth minister, "Tell me what to do now. I feel so lost and hopeless."

We wanted to know how the sense of powerlessness and hopelessness affects all our kids, not just Laurie. Without some sense of control or mastery, one believes that one's life is doomed. Forces outside the self appear to determine the flow of events. Thinking fatalistically, the youth becomes passive and feels no responsibility. "Everything is written." Whatever happens was "meant to be."

How can we identify teens who have slipped into this fatalistic view of life? Researchers and psychologists have identified specific characteristics of people with fatalistic perceptions. These characteristics are listed below:

- *Closed-mindedness*—they often lack openness, flexibility and receptivity to new ideas.
- *Poor reasoning*—they do not process information in a way that illuminates the causes and effects of events in their lives.
- *Lack of assertiveness*—they tend to be followers and find it difficult to accept leadership positions; their apprehension and timidity preclude their taking an assertive stance.
- *Vulnerability*—because they typically see themselves as victims of circumstance, they are vulnerable to exploitation.
- *Poor stress management skills*—particularly under transitional stress and change (common to adolescence), fatalists lack adaptation skills.
- *High ethnocentrism*—they evaluate their peer group as more important than others and do so in a manner that depreciates others.

How can we minister to these teens who have feelings of powerlessness? Christianity is a great antidote to feelings of fatalism. Parents and teachers of teens can do much to articulate the "power" through faith to make life choices. They can also do more to inoculate children against negative media messages, with which they are constantly barraged. Parents and leaders of teens must endlessly reiterate the truth that life in the Spirit is a life of "power," "love," "self-control" and "freedom" (2 Timothy 1:7; Galatians 5:1,22,23).

Even though Christianity teaches a concept of "bond-age" or "slavery" to God in which our wills are renounced or even destroyed, we must also articulate clearly the paradox rooted in this spiritual truth—namely, that the renunciation of self is perfect freedom and spiritual liberty. Christianity does not make people into mindless robots or holy androids. Instead, true submission to God brings power and freedom: "Where the Spirit of the Lord is, there is freedom" (2 Corinthians 3:17). However, the power is not self-generated. It is the gift of God.

Teens who feel a sense of freedom and power over their lives (i.e., those who are "internally controlled" as we define the concept in our survey) live on a higher moral plane than those who feel controlled by others (i.e., those who feel "externally controlled"). Almost a 20 percent higher virginity rate exists among those who feel in control compared to the fatalists (79 percent vs. 60 percent)!

Adolescents with a strong sense of control over their destinies are much more willing to risk the disapproval of peers and friends in order to act according to their own consciences. On the other hand, teens who feel that luck, fate or other persons are in control often unconsciously make themselves victims. They are therefore more likely to be sexually active as well because the voice within tells them that they have no control. "Be careful how you look at the world; it's like that," we recall.

Every person concerned with the welfare of adolescents must understand this fundamental point: Feeling power and control in one's life is essential to a healthy existence. Although considerable attention has been given recently to the importance of building self-esteem in children, we have neglected to promote the equally important value of teaching children the strategies through which they can exercise control over their lives. If we teach our children proper self-esteem but fail to arm them with the skills to live as independent, discerning adults, then we have not adequately equipped them.

Rick and June, the parents of extraordinary children, embrace a very distinct philosophy. They believe that the goal of parenting is to lead children to a personal faith in God, which includes a strong sense of autonomy and independent decision making. The parents spent a good portion of those early years affirming their children, helping them develop a healthy sense of values, and teaching the importance of good decision making. They carefully placed their kids in situations appropriate to their ages and levels of maturity, in which each child had to make decisions. As a result, they reared five children able to stand against the tides of the popular culture.

All of the children grew up knowing they could meet challenges, even of the unknown. One of their sons, Ned, was an outstanding athlete at the local high school, but early in his athletic career, he was faced with a moral dilemma. In Ned's high school, to be accepted as a "real" athlete, one had to lose his virginity. The club's silent motto was "no virgins allowed." Realizing the situation, Ned stood before his entire team one day and said, "I know what you guys expect, but I know what my faith and my parents expect, and I have decided what's best for me. I'll have none of this." The team was astounded, but years later, his reputation is high, and his story has been told in positive terms. What is more, the team let him into the club.

Implications

So what are the spiritual implications for parents, ministers and church leaders? If perceptions do indeed affect our children so drastically, if self-acceptance is closely linked to moral behavior, and if teens with an "internal locus of control" are less likely to be victims at the hands of others, what are we to do? Simply stated, we have to empower our kids, or, more precisely, we must lead them to submit to the Power that can enable them to withstand hostile assaults.

We have three basic tasks before us: we must teach our children sensible coping skills and the discernment to escape dangerous situations; we must lead our children to become independent and autonomous adults capable of choosing wisely without the props of parents and other authorities; and we must teach the essential worth and dignity of every person, based upon a divine evaluation, not a humanistic one.

Teaching Coping Skills

First, our children must acquire some basic coping skills to avoid unnecessary temptation. Joseph was a righteous youth serving in Potiphar's house, but if he had not known when and how to escape the lure of a seductive woman, he would have displeased God. The book of Proverbs is designed partly as instruction to youths about how to avoid unnecessary sexual temptation. The father offers practical wisdom to his sons: "Now then, my sons, listen to me; do not turn aside from what I say. Keep to a path far from her [the adulteress], do not go near the door of her house" (Proverbs 5:7,8).

In concrete and practical ways, we also need to teach our youth how to spot and avoid dangerous situations. In today's warped culture flight from evil may seem cowardly, but it is not. Fleeing from evil is a sign of spiritual maturity and a frequent theme of Bible stories.

We have said much in this chapter about teaching coping skills to our children. We have argued that adolescents should be self-directed. They should feel a measure of control over their lives. In saying these things we must stress that we are not recommending some naive self-help psychology in which youths are exhorted to "believe in themselves" or to "think positively." Rather, we are recommending instruction and modeling, which proclaim individual responsibility in the world. We must teach our children that they do have a measure of power. They do have options. Most important, they can call on divine resources for help. All is not decided. The plots of their lives have not yet been written. In fact, God reserves a future full of hope for them (Jeremiah 29:11).

We are not in sympathy with the humanistic "human potential" way of thinking when we urge our adolescents to take charge of their lives. Yes, adolescents are called to be *self*-disciplined and *self*-controlled (Proverbs 5:23; Titus 2:6). God blesses people who act righteously. On the other hand, righteous actions—seen correctly—are also the work of God. Indeed, self-control is a fruit of the Spirit (Galatians 5:22), the result of divine leading, not the product of psychological muscle-flexing.

The call, then, is not simply to "do more" and "be more" (Believe in yourself! Like yourself! Think positively!), but to yield to the power of God. God calls us to empty ourselves so that He may fill us up. This paradox stands at the heart of the gospel—that the confession of weakness is the beginning of strength, that servanthood is fully liberating. The slave of God is the only truly free person.

If a person is under the sway of God's direction, is he then "inner directed"? For the purposes of our study, yes, definitely. (When speaking of an omnipresent God, "inside" and "outside," "internal" and "external" motivation become meaningless categories.) The God who fills all in all, who is nearer to us than we are to ourselves, in St. Augustine's words, is always both "internal" and "external" to the human self. Perhaps we should simply confess that the categories of social science are grossly inadequate to measure the mysteries of God's operations in the world.

The point is, when adolescents feel this sense of power—whether it is seen as deriving directly from some spiritual force "outside" the self, or whether it is seen as deriving from the "internal" self (which has been touched, converted or moved in some way by a spiritual power)—the outcome is the same in behavioral terms. The inescapable fact is that adolescents resist sexual temptation more easily when they feel the power and "freedom" to resist, however one describes the source of that power.

Teaching Autonomy

Second, we must teach our children to move from dependency to autonomy, that is, to true maturity. Ultimately, moral behavior is not the product of an all-seeing supervisor or a controlling parent. True morality is the product of wise choosing, self-choosing. Teaching teens internal motivation is one of the most precious gifts parents can give children. According to our research, internal motivation is fundamental to ethical behavior.

When we correlated all of the items on internal and external motivation with such categories as virginity, avoidance of intimate touching, and avoidance of pornography, the results were consistent. Simply stated, the principle is this: Those with an internal locus of control have a higher degree of moral behavior, are more consistent with Scripture, accept parental values and avoid the sexual excesses of our culture.

How do children move from dependency to autonomy? In great part this growth takes place because of conscious parental planning. Mothers and fathers must commit themselves to granting increasing measures of freedom and responsibility at every stage of development. These measures of freedom must be appropriate to the age and maturity of the child, and the path to freedom must be rigorously followed even when the parent would find it easier and more convenient to intervene and decide for the child.

At birth a child is totally dependent on the parents, but slowly dependency has to be replaced by self-reliance. By the time a child is ready to leave the family, the child should be able to make individual decisions about matters such as sexual behavior. This goal is not easy to achieve. One mother recently said, "We didn't have our children to let them go. We had our children in order to love them, and that naturally makes us want to keep them." However, the day comes when nurturing must give way to "launching." The child is finally a young adult who must make his or her way in the world. Knowing the right method and day for launching can be difficult, even anguishing, but it can be reached with thought, prayer, and a commitment to the goal of autonomy. The comforting prison-like security of the cocoon must be abandoned for the freedom of flight.

Teaching Divine Worth

Finally, parents must teach their children that they are persons of infinite worth with freedom to choose. A real sense of worth does not come from perpetual pep talks about how "wonderful" or "great" a child is. It derives from specific biblical teaching and parental modeling. The biblical understanding of human worth is imperative.

Paul's letter to Titus provides an interesting context for understanding how to build esteem that leads to moral integrity. Titus is obviously ministering to a congregation of young people and adults who are struggling with various passions. Paul exhorts Titus to teach self-control to young and old alike (2:2-15). The apostle, however, understands, even identifies himself with, those members in their fleshly struggles. "At one time we too were . . . deceived and enslaved by all kinds of passions and pleasures," he writes (3:3). Paul's capacity to understand and recall what others are experiencing is worth noting.

The apostle calls all Christians, young and old, to a high moral life by reminding them of the experience of God's grace in their lives. On the one hand, Paul gives precise instructions to behave properly. On the other, he recalls that it is "the grace of God" (2:11), and not human deeds of righteousness (3:5), that makes people right with God. "For the grace of God . . . teaches us to say 'No' to ungodliness and worldly passions, and to live self-controlled, upright and godly lives in the present age" (2:11,12).

Paul also teaches that a great motivational power for right living comes in knowing the Lord as Redeemer. Christ "gave himself for us to redeem us," and that makes us "eager to do what is good" (2:14). When one contemplates and savors God's grace and when one fathoms that God chooses us and purifies us "for himself a people that are his very own," then motivation for righteous living naturally follows.

The purchase price determines the value of an object. This fact is just as true in matters of faith as it is in the marketplace. If our souls cost the blood of Christ, then we are indeed persons of unimaginable worth! With this understanding the grace of God teaches our youth that they are of great worth—Christ gave Himself for us. Paul implies that a thorough understanding of redemption through the cross is the most powerful motivation to ethical living. We are deeply loved; we are bought with a price. Out of humble gratitude for God's amazing grace, Christians live holy lives. Can one fathom the cross and live unethically? Hardly.

A corollary to the dignity of humans is their innate capacity to make moral choices, that is, to be free. Persons created in God's image have the power to say yes or no. Contrary to the words of the secular tune, people are more than "dust in the wind," tossed by blind cosmic forces. Our parenting strategies ceaselessly must remind our young that they are worthy and capable persons with a future. What they think, say and do matters greatly. They are not property or numbers or nameless faces. They are persons loved and known by God, created for freedom. Not surprisingly, teens in our survey who think in these terms lead more ethical lives.

One thing we can be sure of: Adolescents who feel worthless or powerless do not come by these attitudes accidentally. Feelings of fatalism are primarily "group-rooted"; that is, they are learned within a specific culture or family. Consequently, young people naturally grow up having the same perspective as the groups to which they belong, whether peers, parents or even congregation. Therefore, it is necessary to ask: Do family members see themselves as people of power, governed by God, and able to accomplish goals? Equally important, we must ask: Does the church see itself as a people of leaven and light, able through God's power to touch the world, and willing to take risks for the gospel?

We can hardly expect morally courageous young people to come from homes or congregations paralyzed by despair, pessimism or defeatism. Once again, we perceive a link between family, church and teenager. The spirit of one inevitably impinges on the other.

Conclusion

This study of adolescent perceptions should cause a fresh examination of our outlook as a church. What are our stories, and what do they say about our hope for a future? What are the unstated themes of our discourse? Have fatalistic themes, perhaps unwittingly, permeated our preaching, our lessons and our periodicals? We should scrutinize the stories that we recite among ourselves, for they betray unmistakable themes, either of despair or of hope for the future. This matter is critical because our children absorb the content of our stories and act accordingly.

If we are living by faith, our stories will convey a blessing of inestimable worth to our children. These young people will learn from our words and our deeds that we can do all things through a mighty Christ. They will learn that we are people of faith and hope. They will learn that we are visionaries who can act boldly. "For God did not give us a spirit of timidity, but a spirit of power, of love and of self-discipline" (2 Timothy 1:7). Of all people on the earth, Christians are people with a future. Among such people, our children naturally will find it easier to choose wisely and to live morally courageous lives.

Perception, Jesus taught us, has everything to do with spirituality. The Pharisees and even the disciples failed repeatedly to see the realities of the kingdom and so were in constant spiritual danger. "Though seeing, they do not see; though hearing, they do not hear or understand" (Matthew 13:13). Could this also be our problem and the root problem of our children?

As spiritual leaders of the home and the church, we must hunger to see our youth as they truly are, and we must aspire to lead them to see themselves with God's perspective. As our teen-agers encounter intense sexual temptation, our ministry must be to show them in the deepest sense possible that they are persons of infinite worth and, through God's aid, people of superior strength. Nouwen is correct in writing, "Ministry is the spiritual act of seeing and helping others see the face of a loving God even where nothing but darkness seems to be present." If our children are to make order out of the turbulent chaos of sexual passion, we must help them see that they are loved, valuable and capable beings, created in God's image.

CHAPTER
3

PERSONAL FAITH
AND COMMITMENT

"I have come to the conclusion that a true Jew is not the man who is merely a Jew outwardly, and real circumcision is not just a matter of the body. The true Jew is one who belongs to God in heart, a man whose circumcision is not just an outward physical affair but is a God-made sign upon the heart and soul, and results in a life not for the approval of man, but for the approval of God" (Romans 2:28,29, Phillips).

"To love you have to climb out of the cradle, where everything is 'getting,' and grow up to the maturity of giving, without concern for getting anything special in return. Love is not a deal, it is a sacrifice. It is not marketing, it is a form of worship."—Thomas Merton, Love and Living

---

The Role of Personal Faith

Every system, philosophy or religion eventually faces its "moment of truth." Does Marxism work in the marketplace? Does Einstein's physics correspond to the newest scientific data?

For Christianity, an eminently ethical religion, one necessary test is revealed in a few simple questions: Does its theology translate into changed behavior? Does the Christian faith make a difference in the lives of its adherents? More specifically in the context of this book, does personal faith alter one's sexual behavior? If the answer is no, then our faith system, however "true" in appearance, is ultimately fraudulent. If the Word is not incarnated in the lives of believers and if doctrine does not become deed, then Christianity is suspect.

For this reason, we are saddened by stories of Christians whose behavior and theology are disjointed. Consider Duane and Maryanne, respected children in two very active Christian families. When a youth minister came to serve the congregation, Duane and Maryanne were the first to step forward to help plan retreats, weekly devotionals and other activities. They quickly earned the trust of peers, parents and the youth minister. However, it came to light within a few months that the couple had been sexually involved for more than a year, most of their sexual activity occurring after the weekly devotionals. As the couple later admitted, the devotional time stirred a distorted sense of passion, which led to sexual intimacy after almost every one of the devotionals. In fact, their secret came to light when, following a devotional, someone found them engaged in sexual intercourse in a prayer room they had designed!

How does one explain such behavior? Simply saying that we need to teach the rules of behavior more insistently is not helpful; the incident with Duane and Maryanne occurred in a theologically conservative congregation where rules were clearly emphasized. The problem is not primarily the failure to articulate the biblical guidelines. Rather, it seems that we have managed to emphasize the external requirements without really teaching purity of heart. Something deeper and more central to the Christian faith needs to be instilled, something beyond "the rules."

Perhaps we should begin by confessing our failure to see how God's will should permeate the public and the private self. Perhaps we have failed to convey to our youth that faith is "not just an outward physical affair" but a matter of the heart and soul (Romans 2:28,29). Perhaps we have failed to teach and to show through our own lives that true Christianity is pre-eminently a religion of the Spirit, not the letter.

In our hurry to see adolescents embrace Christianity, we naturally celebrate the external signs that our children have adopted the forms of faith, but we should be more concerned to assess the degree to which they have adopted the internal essences of faith. The most basic issue is this: Do our young people have a deeply personal faith in God?

Our research shows that such a genuine faith commitment is the single most important quality in coping successfully with sexual temptation. As important as baptism, family communication, good preaching, dynamic youth programs, or a dozen other factors are, nothing is as important as personal faith. This fact is clearly illustrated in what our teens tell us about their spiritual lives and their sexual behavior.

Personal Faith and Sexuality

Very significantly, those with a high degree of personal faith are more than twice as likely to be virgins than those with little faith. When personal faith is correlated with virginity, 77 percent of those who had high personal faith were virgins compared to 29 percent who had little personal faith. Another important fact emerges: Some faith is better than none at all. Virginity rates plunge as personal faith decreases

- Faith very helpful   79%
- Faith somewhat helpful   67%
- Faith occasionally helpful 55%
- Faith not at all helpful   29%

Thus we see that those lacking a religious commitment are most at risk.

How then does one explain the case of Duane and Maryanne? Did they have a personal faith? Despite all the external indicators, the answer is no. Both sets of parents were extremely authoritarian and demanding; Duane's and Maryanne's "faith" was their parents', not their own. Even while everyone applauded the children's exemplary obedience and their volunteering to lead youth activities, an internal quality of the Spirit was sadly missing. In truth, their dutiful compliance with parental wishes only masked deep frustration. Their sexual misbehavior was actually covert rebellion, an expression of repressed anger.

In fact, two deeper issues were at play in the prayer room that day. One is passive aggression, that is, the couple's indirect and subtle ways of expressing frustration over excessive parental control. The second issue, for the young woman at least, was the search for genuine affection. Maryanne was longing to feel loved. In the arms of a lover she found a way to receive feelings of worth and acceptance, which she never felt from her father.

Just as personal faith makes a difference in virginity, it also affects the frequency with which adolescents resort to intimate touching. Among those who report a high personal faith in God, almost 30 percent stated they have avoided intimate forms of touching. However, that number drops to 8 percent among adolescents with a low degree of personal faith. Personal faith is a major deterrent to inappropriate erotic behavior.

Personal faith also affects teen-agers' attitudes toward pornography. Sixty percent of those who find personal faith helpful in sexual struggles avoid pornography, but only 26 percent among those lacking personal faith avoided pornography. When it comes to excessive exposure to pornography (viewing it at least once a week), the differences are dramatic. Three percent of those who find personal faith helpful are excessively exposed to pornography compared to 22 percent of those who did not find personal faith helpful. We are struck by the fact that teens who lack a deep personal faith are *seven times* more likely to be excessively exposed to pornography than teens with a deep personal faith.

In summary, we find that *personal faith in God is the most important predictor of adolescent sexual behavior.* The role of personal faith in teen-age behavior is consistent across every major analysis conducted in the study. If we are truly concerned about our youth in sexual crisis, then our most urgent task is to find ways to help them develop an authentic personal faith in God. Certainly we should devote ourselves to understanding the ways in which a lasting, personal, "owned" faith is acquired.

Baptism and Sexuality

Personal faith is an exciting subject, for it represents the internalization of God's teaching. Historically, however, we have viewed baptism as the most decisive expression of personal faith. But is this trust in baptism as the certain sign of a changed life justified? If we were to isolate baptism ·as a factor, would it predict sexual behavior as powerfully as personal faith in God? The answer is no.

Strangely, adolescent baptism is one of the few non-statistical predictors of morality. In other words, the fact that a person has been baptized is no indicator that his or her sexual ethic is superior to one who has not been baptized. When we examine those who have been baptized and those who have not, we find that both groups have identical virginity rates (72 percent). Similarly, technical virginity rates are similar: 71 percent of baptized teens have engaged in intimate touching compared to 75 percent of the unbaptized—an insignificant difference, statistically speaking.

We did find one important difference, however: 20 percent of the baptized say they accept parental values, but only 11 percent of the unbaptized do so. Nonetheless, baptism *by itself* does not singularly impact sexual behavior, according to our findings. Baptism's limited effect on ethical behavior introduces a most significant point of discussion (perhaps reminiscent of Paul's instruction in Romans 6:1-14 and Colossians 2:20–3:10). Christians have commonly viewed baptism as a rite of passage, a spiritual rebirth, an important symbol of faith marking the beginning of an intensely moral and worthwhile life. How then does one explain the similar virginity rates among those who have and who have not been baptized?

Perhaps adolescents view baptism through much different lenses than parents and church leaders. It is altogether possible for young people to accept the importance that the religious community places on the rite of baptism without comprehending the spiritual meaning behind it and without a clear commitment of heart and soul. For some teens, baptism may not be a dramatic new birth involving regeneration and a necessary change in one's moral life. The act may be only a perfunctory institutional requirement. Some see baptism as what you have to do for admission to the ecclesiastical club.

Other explanations may be given for the unchanged lives of the baptized. The first explanation concerns the lack of "cognitive readiness" by which we mean the adolescent's inability to understand and respond to God's truths. Some youths may not be cognitively—or spiritually—ready to understand regeneration. They are asked to "die to self" when they may not have formed or found the "self." Other adolescents have not separated from their parents and are unable to distinguish between parents' wishes and God's wishes. They may find themselves submitting to baptism in an effort to please Mom or Dad, not out of any sense of answering God's call. Indeed, they may confuse their parents' wishes and desires (even if unspoken) and God's loving call. This problem is greatest in homes where parents exercise excessive control and where personal choice and autonomy are depreciated. The result may be compliance, not authentic conversion.

Adolescents are also particularly vulnerable to peer pressure. A good friend, indeed, can be God's way of introducing Christ. However, rather than being an individual decision, baptism often can be a response to group pressure.

No doubt, we also have failed to teach baptism as a genuine death and rebirth into a new life. Having so emphasized the form and the necessity of the act, we may have failed to introduce the *Person* behind the ritual—the Christ and the Spirit who really empower the believer and motivate changes in thought and deed. For some teens, baptism is a hollow ceremony substituting for genuine submission to a living Lord.

Baptism needs to be reframed. It must be seen as the doorway to the living Christ (not the destination), as the entry to a new saving relationship (not a saving act by itself), and as a preliminary act of submission to a living Lord—the first of a lifelong chain of submissive acts before the Master. Christianity is not a discrete point but a continuum, not a locus but a long path. In the words of Eugene Peterson, Christianity is "a long obedience in the same direction."

Finally, the contradiction of unchanged lives may be explained partially by the church's lethargy. Adolescents are affectively oriented, which means they are pre-eminently emotional beings. What must they think when they witness a baptism, this paramount moment when the angels are alleged "to be rejoicing in heaven," yet all they see in the congregation is a wasteland of indifference? "Where is the excitement in the community of faith?" they ask. Where is the sense of celebration over the lost son who has been found? Where is the fatted calf? the joy? the robe? the ring? Why are baptisms not moments of high drama and great celebration?

Adolescents judge the worth of events affectively. But instead of these signs of joy, they may see sleepy-headed adults, preoccupied with the length of the sermon, anxious to arrive at the cafeteria early, or desperate to make the kickoff for the big game. We don't know everything teen-agers think, but this we know: They are unimpressed by spiritual lethargy. They will not buy an incongruent message.

Of course baptism is important to God's plan. But has it lost its meaning? This question is troublesome because adult immersion has been a key to our religious identity. Can God use these findings to restore the richness, the excitement and the vibrancy of baptism? Or will adolescents continue to mirror the apathy of their parents? As no stream rises above its source, neither can we expect our children to hold a higher view of conversion and baptism than is normal in today's church.

Parental Baptism and Teen Sexuality

Does parental baptism have any bearing on adolescent sexuality? We think so. For example, the children of baptized parents have a 75 percent virginity rate compared to a 55 percent rate among the children of unbaptized parents. Among children of unbaptized parents, only 15 percent had avoided intimate touching compared to 27 percent for children of baptized parents.

What causes this difference? The statistics may simply indicate that the children of active church members, which baptism suggests, are more likely to be chaste than the children of non-members. Baptism is an essential requirement for active involvement in churches of Christ. The baptized parents are, by definition, the only ones who can be actively involved. What we may be measuring with this question about baptized parents is church involvement. Obviously, unbaptized parents are not involved in church life, but many baptized parents are involved in many ways. We may surmise that this parental involvement has positive effects on the children.

Once again, it appears that adolescents are more likely to take faith seriously when the adults in their lives do the same. In our worry over so many details of church life, such as Bible school curriculum, dynamic preaching, and exciting youth activities, we may miss the most obvious principle of how children come to know God—through parental commitment. It is a sadly naive strategy to send Allie or Jason off to Sunday school without the parents personally showing them God's way through the family. On the other hand, when parents demonstrate an integrated, deeply personal faith, adolescents are not only impressed, but they are far more likely to follow in their parents' steps.

Religious Commitment and Sexuality

We also asked questions about adolescents' basic religious commitment. Those who have high religious commitment are significantly less at risk than others. Eighty-two percent of the very religiously committed are virgins compared with 43 percent of those who have low or no religious commitment. We also find that less than 1 percent of those with high religious commitment engage in permissive behavior compared to more than 18 percent of those who have little or no religious commitment. Religious commitment is a major factor in helping teens face sexual struggles.

Next, we analyzed religious commitment and its statistical relation to technical virginity and sexual intentions on a date. Of those who profess a high religious commitment, 34 percent avoid intimate touching compared to only 19 percent who profess low or no religious commitment. The data indicate that only 1 percent of those who have high religious commitment intend to be sexually permissive on a date compared with 17 percent of those who have low religious commitment. This comparison shows a notable difference indeed.

Concerning pornography, we find that 69 percent of those who are religiously committed avoid pornography compared with 37 percent of those not religiously committed. The difference becomes more pronounced when one looks at those who use pornography excessively (defined in this study as once a week or more). Among these teen-agers, only 1 percent describe themselves as highly committed compared with 16 percent of those who have no religious commitment.

The pattern is consistent. Just as personal faith in God predicts higher morality, so does religious commitment. Specifically, young people without religious commitment are more than twice as likely to be sexually active before marriage. In some areas of danger (pornography usage, for example), the risks are greater several times over.

Attendance, Attitudes and Sexuality

We will see in Chapter 7 that attendance at religious services is closely linked to positive sexual behavior, but even more important is the adolescent's *attitude* about attending church meetings. Among adolescents who prefer being in church, an 82 percent virginity rate occurs compared to a 52 percent virginity rate among those who do not want to be present. Among those who prefer to attend, 33 percent avoid intimate touching compared to 15 percent who do not want to be present.

Religious commitment also seems to affect teenagers' desires to live consistently with Scripture, just as it affects their attitudes toward pornography and their intentions on a date. Sixty-five percent of the highly religious teens claim consistency with Scripture compared to only 21 percent who have low or no religious commitment. Also, as one might expect, kids who like to be in church generally avoid pornography more than others: 64 percent of those who want to be at church avoid pornography, while only 39 percent of those who dislike attending church avoid pornography. Among those who really want to be at church, 2 percent intend to be sexually permissive on a date. However, youths who really dislike being in church are six times more likely to intend to be sexually permissive on a date (13 percent).

If we wish to know whose moral life is most in danger, we simply have to find out who enjoys church and who doesn't. Those who dislike the experience of church are much more at risk.

Suggestions for Building Faith

To summarize, absolutely nothing can substitute for the adolescent's personal religious faith in coping with sexual temptation. Personal conviction and commitment are vitally important predictors of pure sexual attitudes and behavior. Our research reaffirms what Jesus taught so insistently: What defiles comes from within, not from without (Matthew 15:18). Hence, it should be no surprise that the questions that best reveal the heart's commitment also predict the sort of behavior that naturally will follow.

More than ever, we need to teach a religion of the heart. More than ever, we need to affirm the spirit over the letter, the essence over the form, and internal devotion over lip service. Our preaching, teaching and parenting must conspire to affect the inner being of our children, not only their behavior.

How does one lead adolescents to a committed life? How does one build a life of faith? Here are some suggestions.

First, religious commitment must be founded on security. When children learn to feel safe and know they will not be betrayed, then they are more likely to blossom as adolescents capable of a true personal relationship with God. They also will be less tempted by illicit sex. For many teens, the essential lure of sex is not its pleasure, but its seeming promise of security. A child who does not know trust in her life is ripe for sexual exploitation. Children flourish best in a trusting environment, and no better way exists to develop confidence and security than through the parent/child relationship. Although children acquire feelings of trust and security in many ways, especially through family members, they also acquire these feelings from others, such as a trustworthy baby-sitter or a close friend who guards their secrets faithfully.

Second, a teen-ager is more likely to commit herself to God when she grows up knowing the meaning of a pledge. A pledge is a kind of contract or covenant between two or more people. Implied in a contract or a covenant is the obligation and responsibility to fulfill one's promises at all costs. In a culture where contracts are broken lightly and vows are forgotten easily, we should not be surprised that young adults find commitments difficult to sustain. A child who knows nothing about faithfulness in temporal matters or the adolescent who sees obligations easily cast aside may find it extraordinarily difficult to commit herself to a Father God who demands specific obligations.

Third, the capacity to commit oneself to God grows best in the soil of family loyalty. When this loyalty is missing, tragic consequences are in store. A father recently told his wayward son, "You better cut your hair right now, or I will kick you out of the house." The adolescent's response was equally sharp: "I'll never cut my hair. I have decided I am not obligated to anyone but myself." Whatever the fault of the child, the parent is committing a greater one in so quickly rejecting his son. How can an adolescent learn loyalty toward others if he hasn't first seen it demonstrated toward him?

A precise parallel is seen between this situation and God's treatment of mankind. The parent—whether earthly or divine—must always initiate the love relationship: "We love because he first loved us" (1 John 4:19; cf. Romans 5:8). The parent must show the way. Before the child commits himself to God, he should experience in the family the full meaning of loving obligation. The child who has experienced this sort of loyalty can more easily say, "I want to please because God is my spiritual master, and I want to be His servant."

Through the experience of parental security, trust and loyalty, the child develops a willingness to be bound to God. We are not saying that children lacking these spiritual nutrients are doomed to reject God, but their route to God is often sadly troubled and difficult. Children deprived of a sense of security and significance, especially in early life, may remain emotionally dwarfed; sometimes they simply may be unable to commit themselves to others—whether God or humans.

In short, the children who aren't given security are forever trapped within their own egos. Ever longing for escape, they are never quite able to achieve it in any lasting way. Unfortunately for such persons, casual sex often becomes the escape route of choice— tantalizing and tragically illusory.

Parents who model loving trust, commitment and obligation and who thereby confer significance and worth are doing something priceless for their children. They are teaching their children the only way to escape the cell of narcissism. The wise parent knows that the "freedom" of the infant's cradle soon turns into a terrible prison for the adult. Thomas Merton has written:

> But the plain truth is this: love is not a matter of getting what you want. Quite the contrary. The insistence on always having what you want, on always being satisfied, on always being fulfilled, makes love impossible. To love you have to climb out of the cradle, where everything is 'getting,' and grow up to the maturity of giving, without concern for getting anything special in return. Love is not a deal, it is a sacrifice. It is not marketing, it is a form of worship.[1]

Children who do not learn the joy and the mystery of family love may turn into adults who futilely try to escape themselves through empty, short-lived sexual encounters. They find making commitment to another, whether human or God, to be difficult.

Perhaps this is why religion, sexual behavior and family life are so closely linked in Scripture. Isn't a healthy relationship with God, described in the Bible in metaphors of extraordinary intimacy, very much like family love and married love? Isn't the failure of one kind of love relationship mirrored in other relationships (fornication = spiritual infidelity = idolatry)? So it appears in Scripture; so it seems today.

As we consider the sexual problems of our teens, we must be diligent to cut through the surface and secondary issues to find the deepest problems that plague our children, that indeed plague all of us. Ultimately the issues are "heart" problems, problems of shallow love and half-hearted commitment, in ourselves and in our families.

No sexual problems face our teens today that faith cannot solve. While the fires of sensual passion seem overwhelming at times, the fact is that an even greater force is available to the believer—the fire of divine love.

What motivates high ethical behavior? Above all, the motivation is a personal relationship with a divine being, a relationship that can be made comprehensible by the experience of a healthy family environment. The love of family ultimately witnesses to the greatest power known to humans—the Father's love expressed in Christ. "The very spring of our actions is the love of Christ," says Paul. "The love of Christ controls us" (2 Corinthians 5:14 NASB). If we are to succeed with our youth, this great reality is the beginning and the ending of our message and our ministry.

Endnote

1. Thomas Merton, *Love and Living*, eds. Naomi B. Stone and Patrick Hart (San Diego: Harcourt Brace Jovanovich, 1985), 34.

CHAPTER
4

FAMILY STYLES
AND SEXUALITY

*"For the grace of God . . . teaches us to say 'No'
to ungodliness and worldly passions, and to live
self-controlled, upright and godly lives in this
present age" (Titus 2:11,12).*

*"Cat's in the cradle and the silver spoon,
The little boy blue and the man in the moon.
'When you comin' home, Dad?'
'I don't know when, But we'll get together then,
You know we'll have a good time then.' "
—Harry Chapin, "Cat's in the Cradle"*

Do Families Make a Difference?

When Ellen was 10 years old, she had some questions about "the facts of life." She had heard a strange word on the playground, and she naturally turned to her mother for an explanation. What should have been a simple dialogue about the beauty of human sexuality turned into a scarring memory.

Now, more than 25 years later, Ellen still recalls the consternation in her mother's face when the girl asked the simple question. Ellen's mom refused to say anything at all, but the next day she handed the child a weighty medical book on human reproduction. "Here, read this," she said, offering no advice, no explanation—not even a helpful tip such as "Read Chapter 14."

Ellen, more puzzled than anything, browsed through the book until she found the right section. There she read in cold clinical language what she had asked about the day before. But, Ellen recounts years later: "It sounded horrible. It was shocking! I never wanted to get married. I cried. And I never asked my mother another question about this subject. Never."

Others find it equally difficult to converse with their parents. Alex, a rather enterprising young man, was frustrated by his inability to talk to his very busy dad. So under an assumed name he made an appointment through the secretary at his father's office. When Alex appeared at the office door at the arranged time, his dad said, "Why are you here, Alex? I have an appointment. Sorry." The teen replied, "Dad, I *had* to make an appointment under a different name. We really have to talk."

What is the relationship between teen-age sexual behavior and the willingness of parents to relate to their children in meaningful, healthy ways? If children belong to strongly supportive, understanding families dedicated to authenticity and honesty, our research shows that one can expect a higher level of morality. On the other hand, if children reside in distant, uncommunicative homes where real feelings and needs are masked or denied, we generally can predict lower moral behavior. When families are unwilling to communicate freely and when they are unwilling to support their children and deal frankly with their questions, serious problems are to be expected.

Our study indicates that three critical areas are important predictors of sexual attitudes and behaviors. These areas are parent-child communication styles, family systems, and parental religiosity and values.

FAMILY COMMUNICATION STYLES

Communication is not just a matter of conveying information—"Be home at 8 o'clock; clean your room; I like your new jacket." Family communication is not principally a matter of transmitting data. In families, as in other relationships, the facts being transmitted are often of secondary importance. The greater message is the *fact* of communication itself *because the act of communicating implies a relationship.* Even simple messages such as "Pass the salt" or "Please help me peel the potatoes" are significant because they imply a relationship. The implicit affirmation of the other person, signified by the communication, turns out to be as important as, often more important than, the basic data being transmitted. Communication means, simply, that two or more persons are in relationship.

Hence, teens from uncommunicative families are always in distress. They suffer, not from a lack of information, but from the chronic, haunting fear that they do not live in a meaningful relationship. That is to say, they feel unloved. Silence is truly the deadliest form of communication because it says eloquently, "You do not matter." Silence is death to a relationship.

This being so, it is important to ask questions about the connection between family communication styles and sexual behavior. We asked a series of questions concerning how families communicate on matters of sexuality. The questions allowed us to look candidly inside church families. The survey revealed significant feelings teens have about family communication.

- 71 percent found it difficult to talk.
- 62 percent felt lack of confidence discussing sex.
- 74 percent wanted to avoid talking about sex.
- 58 percent said they, the teens, were scared to talk about sex.
- 45 percent said they did not receive helpful advice from parents.
- 49 percent said their parents did not understand.
- 56 percent said there is rarely or never a good time to talk.

Obviously, responses like these—indicating the presence of fear, anxiety, poor understanding and time pressures—suggest that insufficient information is being shared in the family on several matters. Fortunately, however, what information does squeeze through is perceived by the adolescent as honest; 71 percent of the teens see parents as "honest no matter what." In other words, parental integrity is high. Yet, as God's primary agency through which biblical principles are passed from one generation to another, Christian parents are too silent.

The respondents generally perceive parents as unavailable, unapproachable, unhelpful, unable to understand, and lacking in confidence. We can't tell if these perceptions stem from poor timing of conversations, the awkwardness with which parents conduct discussions, or even parents' discomfort with their own sexuality. The fact is, Christian adolescents are saying that little communication about sex is occurring, but they view as honest the little information that does seep through.

Family Communication and Virginity

Briefly stated, virginity is more likely to be found among adolescents from families with good communication patterns. Five critical aspects of communication between parents and adolescents proved statistically significant in explaining virginity.

(1) Communication avoidance. First, a higher virginity rate exists among those families that look forward to communication about sexuality compared to those families that tend to avoid communication about sex (72 percent vs. 66 percent virginity rate).

Charlene remembers her questions about sex when she was 8 years old. Out of his own discomfort, her father responded, "We don't talk about that here." When she was 9 she was sexually abused by her uncle. She tried again to talk to her father, this time about the uncle's abuse. He only responded, "We don't talk about that here." At 10, she was molested by her grandfather, and once more she heard from her Dad, "We don't talk about that here."

At 34, as a patient in a psychiatric hospital trying to cope with the trauma of a recent rape, Charlene painfully shared four other instances of sexual abuse, and at times she painfully remembers her father saying the same words, "We don't talk about that here." Today, she is a psychotic locked in a fantasy world, in part because of her father's denial.

Contrary to popular thinking, openness about sexual matters in a family context does not encourage sexual experimentation. Knowledge, unshrouding "the secret," is much wiser than wrapping sex in veils of silence. Avoiding communication may be the worst possible strategy. It is far better to be open, direct and non-defensive in talking about sexuality.

(2) Honesty. Another critical area is the adolescent's perception of parental honesty. A significant link is seen between the kind of communication that takes place in the family and adolescent virginity. Higher virginity rates occur among adolescents who perceive parents to be honest (76 percent) vs. adolescents who see parents as dishonest (54 percent).

Frankness and directness produce better adjusted teen-agers because the parents' willingness to communicate establishes a model for teens, enabling them to cope successfully in later years when sexual temptation strikes. They have an established pattern for talking, for sharing their burdens, and for seeking out resources and the comfort of others. Unfortunately, the child from the "silent" home has no such model to help him or her in a time of crisis.

Consider Debby's case. Debby, an attractive daughter of Christian parents, had lived abroad as well as in several large United States cities because of her father's business. She was cosmopolitan and dated frequently, but she was able to handle sexual temptation with relative ease. This ability was so in part because of her close family relationship. Debby had the kind of father who made it easy to discuss almost any topic. Debby and her two sisters learned to deal directly with emotions.

When family secrets about aunts and uncles became an issue, the family was known to have stayed up until 1 or 2 a.m. to talk. They discussed one uncle who had molested a child and another who beat his children. The family also talked about the marital difficulties of people they knew, and they openly discussed the causes of divorce among their acquaintances. Consequently, Debby developed very strong and highly moral attitudes. The family history shows that Debby and her two sisters have maintained a high moral life and are happily married.

So honesty is very important. Of course we are not calling for "brutal honesty," a frankness that can border on cruelty or verbal voyeurism, but we do recommend being true to what has happened and avoiding the secrecy that often characterizes sexual issues in the family.

(3) Anxiety. A third issue concerns parental anxiety. Talking openly about sexuality with your adolescent is one thing; conducting the discussion in a relaxed and comfortable manner is quite another. The degree of comfort in the communication process is quite important. Among the children of "relaxed" parents, there was a higher rate of virginity (73 percent) compared to the children of "anxious" parents (60 percent). Parental anxiety affects parent-adolescent communication; that perceived anxiety, in turn, seems to affect the adolescent's behavior.

When Darren was 14, he asked his parents if kissing was wrong. His father responded with some ambiguous statements on the subject. Darren pursued the matter further by stating that he had been involved in some "deep kissing." At this point, his mother and father became abnormally reserved and tense. Although they continued to talk in general terms about sexuality, everything Darren heard was deeply colored by his parents' anxiety. They failed to give any clear answers to Darren's questions, but they did manage to convey one unspoken point: "We really don't want to talk about this subject."

Darren was confused by this mixed message. On one hand, he thought his parents were encouraging

him to be open. On the other, when he was frank,
their anxiety prevented his being sure about what
they were saying. The result is that he never opened
up to his parents about sexual issues again.

(4) *Availability*. A fourth critical area is parental
availability. We find that among those adolescents
who perceive that their moms and dads are available,
a higher virginity rate occurs. Specifically, the virginity rate among those adolescents with "available"
parents is 74 percent compared with only 59 percent
for others. Some teens apparently believe that there
is never a good time for family discussion; unfortunately, this perception is closely related to a lower
virginity rate. However, another group of teens believes that almost any time is a good time for conversation in their families, and correspondingly, the
virginity rate is higher.

Time management is not always a neat and easy
matter. Parental availability is not simply a matter of
revising calendars and daily schedules. Adolescents—
indeed all children—also demand a measure of emotional availability. Parents may well have an agenda
that leaves little room for real interaction. Wives and
teens frequently describe husbands and fathers who
are physically present, but who are absent in mind
and soul. Like the boy in Harry Chapin's "Cat's in
the Cradle" who is always waiting for the dad to
share his life at some elusive point in the future,
everyone is asking, "When are you coming home,
Dad? When are you coming home?"

Parental unavailability is a pattern that begins much
earlier than adolescence, certainly. Researchers now
are indicating a person's self-worth is deeply rooted
in the circumstances of early childhood. In those early
months and years, the child learns security, a sense
of worth, and trust from parents who lavish attention

and praise. When focused attention is missing, children feel insignificant. One can only imagine the level of self-esteem in the hearts of the children who were surveyed a few years ago when researchers reported that father-child communication averaged only 37 seconds a day!

When parents make children a priority, they are conferring value and meaning on their children's lives, and they are indirectly teaching their offspring that they have *divine* significance. After all, parental attention is a mirror of God's profound love for humankind: "Is not Ephraim my dear son, the child in whom I delight?" God asks. "My heart yearns for him; I have great compassion for him" (Jeremiah 31:20). "When Israel was a child, I loved him. . . . It was I who taught Ephraim to walk, taking them by the arms . . . . It was I who healed them. I led them with cords of human kindness, with ties of love; I lifted the yoke from their neck and bent down to feed them" (Hosea 11:1,3-4).

God is a nurturing, compassionate parent in these passages. Hosea pictures God as a faithful parent, even when Israel was behaving very much like an adolescent. When Israel acted childishly, God responded faithfully, maturely and judiciously. We are called to demonstrate a similar sort of passionate attention toward our children.

(5) Parental helpfulness. A final critical area is parental helpfulness, the advice teens receive from their parents in talking about sex. We find that teens who think their parents give helpful advice have a 75 percent virginity rate compared to a 57 percent rate among teens who view parental advice as unhelpful. A college student in a Bible class on adolescent sexuality commented on the quality of her parents' instructions on sex: "Actually, I don't think I was all

that equipped to deal with teen sexual issues, since the only thing my parents gave me was a book about hamsters." Our teens really do want straightforward answers, and when they choose to listen to parents, they expect accuracy and relevance.

The research confirms that positive communication patterns, such as the five outlined above, contribute to significantly higher rates of virginity. Of course, virginity is not the only measure of adolescent sexuality, but measuring it is one means of determining how our youngsters are faring. If we are going to assist our teens in maintaining their moral lives, then obviously parental communication styles must improve.

Communication Styles and Pornography

A casual drive through most communities or a glance at the local magazine stand or even the television program guide will reveal the prevalence of pornography in the United States today. Yet the assumption among many people, particularly religious people, is that pornography is used by only a handful. That assumption may be true of hard-core pornography as defined by James Dobson and others, but pornography in its various forms, including "soft porn," is very much with us. In our sample, which focused almost entirely on religious people, we found almost half of our respondents (46 percent) have used pornography in some form or another. The frequency varies from two or three times a year all the way to 3 percent who claim to use pornography weekly.

The rates of pornography use can be meaningfully related to family communication patterns. These correlations reveal some significant facts about family communication patterns and pornography.

- Pornography usage is lower in families that provide helpful communication about sexuality compared to families that fail to provide helpful communication (62 percent avoid pornography vs. 46 percent).
- Pornography usage is lower in families that encourage communication and seek opportunities to share (62 percent avoid pornography vs. 53 percent).
- Usage is lower among families where understanding between parent and child is high (59 percent vs. 50 percent).
- Usage is lower when teens consider their parents to be available (69 percent vs. 42 percent).
- Usage is lower when families practice honest, open communication (59 percent vs. 51 percent).

These findings suggest something important that has eluded other researchers. From numerous case studies, counselors have known that pornography usage was linked to family dysfunction, yet reasons for this occurrence were not apparent. Now we can see one of the links: Negative styles of family communication are related to a teen-ager's attraction to pornography. Teens apparently turn to pornography when they lack meaningful relationships at home. Conversely, positive communication styles within families contribute to lowered rates of pornography usage, reducing the risk by as much as 16 percent.

We conclude that ineffective family communication may propel some young people into other forms of undesirable "communication." Healthy families must practice honest and open communication in a supportive, non-defensive climate. If the adolescent believes the climate to be workable, then communication is further enhanced and the acting out of negative behavior is diminished. However, if teen-agers perceive the communication climate to be negative, then we can predict that they will progressively distance themselves from their parents' values.

Communication and Technical Virginity

One may recall from earlier discussions that we asked a number of questions about physical touching as a substitute for sexual intercourse (technical virginity). We found, overall, that only 25 percent of the sample had never practiced intimate touching.

Among those families with strained levels of communication, we learn that there is a higher rate of mutual touching than in families that have good communication patterns. Teens from "silent" families are twice as likely to engage in intimate touching as other teens. Adolescent perception of parental helpfulness is another significant factor. Intimate touching is almost three times more common among teens from families perceived as not helpful (34 percent) compared with teens from "helpful" families (12 percent).

The same pattern is true regarding honesty of communication within the family. Among those families where the parents were perceived as honest when they talked about sex, there was a significantly lower rate of intimate touching (27 percent vs. 19 percent). Even more dramatic is the finding that adolescents from families practicing dishonest communication were almost three times more likely to be involved in intimate touching (32 percent) than teens from families characterized by honest communication (13 percent).

Barbara was a 16-year-old sophomore in a prestigious metropolitan high school. Her father was a high-ranking officer in the military, and the churchgoing family was considered extremely successful. Because Barbara had grown up hearing the usual moral teachings, her parents just assumed that their daughter shared their values. Barbara's mom and dad assumed they had nothing to worry about, and thus they provided very few rules concerning her dating. They allowed her to begin car dating when she was in the eighth grade. However, beneath the smooth appearance of things, there were a number of serious problems. Though Barbara was a technical virgin, preserving her virginity as she saw it, she felt entirely free to engage in heavy petting and various forms of intimacy to satisfy her sexual desires. After all, she could claim that she was a virgin.

Many Christian parents are like Barbara's. Because they like their children and spend time with them and because they vacation together and go to church together, they imagine that they understand one another and that they are communicating well. However, the communication remains superficial, and there is no real meeting of minds.

Summary of Communication Styles

Three lessons may be learned from this research about sexuality and communication styles.

First, the communication must be two-way. If communication is only one-way, where parents talk and kids listen, teen-agers are certain to view the message (however true) as negative and demeaning. Inevitably they will feel inadequate and powerless.

A second lesson to be gleaned is that listening can be a greater ministry than speaking. Listening is, in fact, the most important variable in the communication process. Listening is creative and healing; it provides a climate in which all persons in the group can be received as persons of infinite worth.

If young people believe their opportunity to be heard is thwarted, they are likely to quit responding to their parents. "I don't care," they say aloud, but they do care immensely. Inwardly they say to themselves, "I don't count." These are the youths most likely to turn to pornography or sex. Parents must train themselves to listen deeply and at length. All parents should consider Dietrich Bonhoeffer's counsel:

> Anyone who thinks that his time is too valuable to spend keeping quiet will eventually have no time for God and his brother. . . . Christians have forgotten that the ministry of listening has been committed to them by Him who is Himself the great listener and whose work they should share. We should listen with the ears of God that we may speak the Word of God.[1]

Parents must be inclined to listen to their children at almost any time. Communication in the family is not something that happens by fate or accident, nor can we afford to wait for some crisis to bring us together. Rather, we must calculate deliberately to be available. Not every adolescent wants to talk when parents are ready. The happiest circumstance for communication arises when adolescent willingness is blended with parental availability. So, the parents' motto should be the words of Hamlet: "The readiness is all."

The last lesson is that communication provides an instructional model for adolescents, a picture and a permission. Good family communication presents a picture to teen-agers; it shows them possibilities for handling later difficulties and helps them visualize concretely how to talk about their sexual feelings.

When they feel safe to talk freely, as modeled by their parents, they will also feel free to confront themselves or a dating partner when necessary.

In other words, good family communication also provides a kind of permission. When the drives become strong, the boy or the girl may say: "This is inappropriate. Let's talk about this." The family history of open talk liberates the teen from a trap. Hence, we say, good family communication is both a picture and a permission.

FAMILY SYSTEMS AND SEXUALITY

Mary's parents brought her to the counselor's office for help. The mother was extremely angry and embarrassed. She said she wanted her daughter "fixed," for Mary was 14, unmarried and pregnant. Over a period of eight months and with intensive therapy, a massive and complicated story unfolded, not just about Mary, but Mary's family. The story spanned four generations.

The truth is that Mary's mother, her grandmother, and even her great-grandmother (all of whom were named Mary) had been pregnant out of wedlock at precisely the same age—14. Mary's problem was a shared one—"systemic," we say. No longer can we talk about a teen-ager's problems in isolation, as though she were detached and floating somewhere in the universe. We must learn to see our teen-agers' problems in the light of the larger family system.

Mary's story underscores the essential point that the family does not consist of isolated entities. Instead, parents and children function integrally within a group. The family is a tightly woven web or network; to touch one thread is to vibrate the whole. In a healthy family system, then, all members work together to achieve emotional stability. If a father loses his job, the loss is felt throughout the family. If a daughter turns up pregnant, her anxieties resonate throughout the family.

In other words, the family is not a loose assortment of independent elements like the miscellaneous items in a lost-and-found box; it is a body (cf. Romans 12:4; 1 Corinthians 12:14-26). What happens to one affects all.

Family Systems and Virginity

What is the connection between family support-iveness and sexual behavior? We know that some families are extremely supportive in a crisis, and others are not. One father, upon learning of his daughter's pregnancy at age 16, literally abandoned her. He ordered her out of the house and refused to forgive her the rest of his life. Although this is an extreme case, many families take similar, if less dramatic, positions. In great difficulty, some families freeze up and become increasingly distant. Others silently nourish grudges for years, ruling out the possibility of healing.

Our research suggests that the children of support-ive families (and we mean supportive in all circum-stances, not only during a sexual crisis) are far more likely to behave ethically and maturely. Virginity is significantly higher among children from supportive families (76 percent) compared to the children from non-supportive families (61 percent). Children from non-supportive families are twice as likely to be involved in casual or incidental sex (19 percent) compared to the children from supportive families (9 percent).

The inescapable inference is that non-supportive families may unwittingly drive their children into the arms of casual sex. The emotional destitution of the home compels the child to look for psychological food outside the family, often in unsavory and dangerous places. The supreme irony in all this is that some extremely rigid parents are, through their rigidity, actually encouraging the behavior they deplore so deeply.

We also find that children from close or cohesive families have a higher virginity rate than children from homes where closeness or cohesiveness is lacking (79 percent vs. 58 percent). Furthermore, children from loosely knit families are three times more likely to engage in casual sex than the children from closely knit families.

We are certain that an adolescent's perception of the family is crucial in shaping behavior. One might say, "As a child thinks in his heart about his family, so is he." This idea is particularly true when considering an adolescent's perception of whether or not his parents understand him. "Understanding" is a relative matter; nonetheless, adolescents differ in their behavior according to their perception of their parents' capacity to understand. Virginity rates are higher among teens from "understanding" families (77 percent) compared to teens from families viewed as not understanding (52 percent).

Another important issue concerns the management of the family (i.e., the way in which authority and decision making are handled). Respondents were asked to place their family on a scale ranging between "autonomous" and "dictatorial." Very few families fall at either extreme, but most tend in one direction or the other. When ratings on this scale were compared to virginity rates, some intriguing facts emerged. The children from families where autonomy is encouraged clearly do better. They have a 77 percent virginity rate compared to a 57 percent virginity rate for children from autocratic families. When autonomy is discouraged and blind adherence to rules is demanded, young people often are unable to cope with complex or unfamiliar situations later on when the mom and dad are absent. Encouraging children toward more personal responsibility is a wise objective in parenting.

Rules are peculiar things. They should be announced and enforced. But rules must be built on broad principles. When those underlying principles are taught in addition to the rules, our children are more likely to internalize and own what they have been taught. If children are taught to think through reasons why and to weigh and assess concepts and principles beyond the basic prescriptions, then they are more likely to accept individual responsibility for their actions. Our research suggests that children who are taught autonomy will more likely remain morally pure.

Family Systems and Pornography

Similar findings resulted when we looked at pornography usage. Frequent viewers of pornography are up to four and a half times more likely to come from non-supportive homes. On the other hand, teen-agers who enjoy spending time with family members and whose parents encourage them to make independent decisions and to participate in family discussions—in other words, teens from healthy, functional families—use pornography much less than other teens.

It makes sense, doesn't it? If a family is not supportive, is not cohesive, and shows little understanding, then the adolescent must seek support and comfort elsewhere. Some may fill these needs through friendships, but others become reclusive, turning to the fantasy world of pornography, which, for the victim, becomes the new reality. The future for a teen hooked on such material is not bright. That teen's life may be filled with isolation and loneliness. In extreme cases, pornography can become the source of further sexual deviation, and it can become addictive, requiring treatment similar to that used with chemically dependent persons.

Family Systems and Technical Virginity

Rates of technical virginity (intimate touching) can also be correlated to family systems. Adolescents from positive families practice technical virginity less than other teens.

- Adolescents from supportive families avoid intimate touching twice as much as non-supportive families (33 percent vs. 16 percent).
- Adolescents from cohesive families avoid intimate touching two and a half times more than non-cohesive families (26 percent vs. 10 percent).
- Adolescents whose parents encourage independent decision making (autonomy) avoid intimate touching more than teens whose parents discourage independent thought (30 percent vs. 19 percent).
- Adolescents from understanding families avoid intimate touching two and one-half times more than

teens who feel misunderstood (30 percent vs. 13 percent).

One sees the same pattern as in the findings with virginity and pornography. When families are supportive and close and when they encourage individual decision making, then adolescents are less at risk. In other words, the teen-agers who are most tempted to seek sexual intimacy belong to families that find it difficult to affirm the teen-agers' significance and personal worth.

FAMILIES INSPIRING ACCEPTANCE OF VALUES

Every day, dozens—even hundreds—of distractions, visible and invisible, conscious and unconscious, pull at our teen-agers. Our task is not to fret about each one of these ever-present temptations. Rather, God has placed parents in the home to serve as "executives" with the mission to instill moral values and empower children to exercise these values properly. Sometimes parents forget this calling. They should know that regardless of what their children may say or do, *most* of them are slowly, quietly adopting their parents' values.

But how can we be *certain* that our children are adopting our values? How can we lead our children to share our faith? Why do some children adopt parental values more completely and enthusiastically than others (sometimes even within the same family)? No doubt the answers are complex, but the nature of the family system is surely a part of the story. Parents who are concerned about leaving a moral and spiritual legacy should pay particular attention to the quality of their "family system."

Table 4.1 graphically confirms our claim that teenagers are much more likely to adopt their parents' values when the family environment has certain positive features. For example, note the close relationship between positive characteristics in the family system and the child's willingness to accept parental values.

TABLE 4.1

Home Factor	Rate of Acceptance of Parental Values
Home has positive communication climate	48%
Home has negative communication climate	9%
Home has relaxed communication environment	44%
Home has tense communication environment	22%
Teen feels comfortable communicating with parents	37%
Teen feels uncomfortable communicating with parents	5%
Teen feels his or her suggestions are valued	34%
Teen feels his or her suggestions not valued	5%
Home has "high understanding" of teen	53%
Home has "low understanding" of teen	9%
Home encourages acceptance of responsibility	41%
Home doesn't encourage acceptance of responsibility	31%
Decisions almost always discussed with family members	56%
Decisions almost never discussed with family members	13%
Home has open and direct communication environment	59%
Home communication marked by avoidance	18%
Teen feels closest to family members	53%
Teen feels closest to persons outside the family	13%

Home Factor	Rate of Acceptance of Parental Values
Home in which "anytime is a good time to talk"	54%
Home in which "no time is a good time to talk"	11%
Teen receives helpful advice when talking to parents	34%
Teen does not receive helpful advice when talking to parents	6%
Teen feels that parents genuinely listen	49%
Teen feels parents don't genuinely listen	28%
Teen values family cohesiveness	33%
Teen does not value cohesiveness	3%

This list gives parents an agenda on which to focus, and it also gives hope to parents who sometimes become discouraged and doubtful in the short run. These data also remind us that parents are not called to be mechanical moral police officers, spouting do's and don'ts every day; they are called to weave a family fabric that protects and secures each family member in love, not law. Issues like music, clothing styles, peer groups, and curfews—important as these sometimes seem to be—are less vital than a family atmosphere brimming with feelings of ease, psychological safety, belonging, acceptance and respect.

Summary: Three Parental Strategies

How can parents best help children adopt the right values? Above all, parents need to maintain three important qualities that we call availability, approachability and authenticity.

Our research consistently shows the absolute importance of parents' being available. When children get the impression that "anytime is a good time" to talk and share, they will have a greater chance of maintaining moral behavior. By contrast, when children are led to think "there is no time to talk" or that the right times are rare and severely limited, negative sexual consequences are more likely.

"Availability" is more than physical presence. It also includes "emotional readiness," total presence of mind and soul. Availability means not being preoccupied with an adult agenda. Because adolescents are by nature wanting to break away from family, true availability is more a matter of fitting into the schedule of the teen when he or she is ready to talk, rather than the other way around. A busy, preoccupied parent trying to earn a living and keep the household above chaos may find the idea of always being ready to listen whenever the adolescent is ready to talk to be quite demanding, but making the effort is well worth the energy.

"Approachability" means that parents are askable. That is, they convey an implicit spirit and an attitude that says, "It's OK to ask any question, pose any problem, and express any feeling. No issue is off-limits in this family. I won't condemn or rant. I won't even frown or twitch nervously. I will listen with openness and understanding."

The old adage that "Children are to be seen and not heard" may be comforting nostalgia, but adhering to that philosophy is neither good Christianity nor good psychology. A positive family lifestyle means sharing by all—reciprocity in dialogue about sexual issues as in other topics.

Finally, our research suggests the extraordinary power of parental honesty and basic willingness to face situations realistically. Offering platitudes that worked for an earlier generation will not necessarily help today. But silence is equally inadequate. Today's teens often complain, "Our parents give us no advice and no resources; they refuse to talk." It is perplexing when worldly-minded parents equip their children with a single message, "Be smart. Use a condom." But it is tragic when a whole generation of religious parents fails to provide any message at all. How dare we leave our children as orphans, cut off from the biblical message of chastity?

Salvador Minuchen, in his book *Families and Family Therapy*, tells the story of arctic explorer Robert Peary who led various expeditions to the North Pole. On one journey he labored tirelessly all day trying to reach his destination, only to discover that as he approached his intended destination, his compass revealed that he was farther south than when he began his trip. His confusion was resolved when he discovered that he had been traveling on a large iceberg that was drifting south faster than his trek north. Minuchen draws a conclusion: "Man is not himself without his circumstances."[2]

We too are convinced that adolescents cannot be understood apart from the family context. To look at sexual behavior without reference to family dynamics is to view only the dogsled and not the drifting iceberg.

Endnotes

1. Dietrich Bonhoeffer, *Life Together*, trans. John W. Doberstein (New York: Harper and Row, 1954), 98-99.
2. Salvador Minuchen, *Families in Family Therapy* (Cambridge, Mass.: Harvard University Press, 1974), 2, 5.

CHAPTER 5

WHEN FRIENDS MAY BE FOES: PEERS AND SEXUALITY

" 'The Talmud says that a person should do two things for himself. One is to acquire a teacher. Do you remember the other?' —'Choose a friend,' I said."—Chaim Potok, The Chosen

"A friend is a friend at all times, it is for adversity that a brother is born" (Proverbs 17:17).

"Nothing is more disgraceful than a false friendship. Avoid this most of all."—Marcus Aurelius

---

At 14 Olivia seemed the model child in a solid Christian home. She was cheerful, cooperative and responsible at home and at school. But at 15 things began to change. The first signal was her change in friends. She abandoned her friends at church one by one and took up with a totally new set of friends at her large urban high school. Her new friends were the "Low Riders," a group known to use alcohol and drugs.

When her parents talked to Olivia about her change of companions, Olivia became defensive, accusing them of being unsympathetic, ill informed and prejudiced. "What you say is ridiculous," she exclaimed. "I'm not a druggie just because I'm in the Low Riders!" The parents obviously had hit a sensitive nerve. Olivia's anger turned into rage as she screamed, "You don't trust me; you don't trust me. You have never trusted me!" Using the religious ideas she knew so well, she turned on her mother with a final, telling blow: "Besides, you're the one, Mother, who always told me that Christ spent His time with non-Christians."

This one statement immobilized Olivia's mother. As she pondered these words, the mother struggled between rival claims—a strong desire to protect her daughter from evil influences and the equal desire for Olivia to be light in a dark world. Can parents have it both ways?

Every parent sooner or later faces the same question: How does one balance the need for protection with the call to be witnesses in the world? As Christian teens mature and associate with peers holding different values, the issue becomes ever more urgent. Knowing how powerfully friends can influence adolescents, should Christian adolescents have close non-Christian friends? Is it dangerous for their closest friendships to come from outside the circle of faith?

To the Christians in Corinth, Paul offered two answers that must somehow be balanced. On the one hand he cites a familiar proverb, "Do not be misled, 'Bad company corrupts good character' " (1 Corinthians 15:33). The statement seems emphatic and decisive. Parents have recited this kind of wise advice to their children for ages. Marcus Aurelius, an emperor of ancient Rome, gave almost identical counsel: "Nothing is more disgraceful than a false friendship. Avoid this most of all."

However, in the same letter, the apostle writes about an equally compelling obligation. Paul tells Christians not to avoid worldly associations. He writes that Christians should not try to dissociate themselves from the immoral, the greedy, or even idolaters outside the body of Christ, for to do so "you would have to leave this world" (1 Corinthians 5:10). Living in the world means meeting people, working with people, and befriending people who do not share our Christian values. Being a disciple of Jesus means becoming a friend of sinners as did the Master (Matthew 11:19). Christians are faced with the difficult calling of being friends *in* the world without being friends *of* the world.

How is this to be done? Can friendships outside the church's walls be wholesome and constructive, or do they necessarily corrupt good morals? Who was right in the family argument, Olivia or her parents? We set out to find answers to these questions by examining the nature of adolescent friendships. What our own teens tell us is most illuminating.

Positive Peer Networks

First, we determined the source of friendships among our respondents. Where do our teens find their friends—in the local congregation, in the larger fellowship of the church, or elsewhere? Are their friends "religious," even if not members of the respondents' congregations? For those who think it imperative that Christian teens have friends who are believers, the news is excellent as the list below shows:

- 31 percent say their close friends come from their home congregations.
- 36 percent say their close friends come from another congregation of the church of Christ.
- 23 percent say their close friends belong to or attend other churches.
- Only 11 percent say their closest friends are non-religious.

To summarize, almost 90 percent of the respondents say that their closest friends are religious. Two-thirds of our youth find their close friends in their home church, and only one in 10 finds his or her primary friendships among non-believers. How did this pattern of friendships among children in church come to be? Is it the natural consequence of our children spending a lot of time in church-sponsored programs? The church's providing activities and programs is surely part of the answer. One of the most pronounced missions of youth and family programs today is the bringing together of young people so that strong friendships will develop. Apparently, this strategy is working. Other influences are having some impact too, including parental guidance, preaching and teaching, and adolescents' internalization of family and congregational values.

Negative Peer Networks

Olivia, the young girl who joined the rowdies at school, fits in the 11 percent of our sample who find their best friends outside the circle of faith. What typically happens to these kids like Olivia who choose to spend their time with the worldly set? Remember that Olivia tried to justify her membership in the group because she said she wanted to be like Jesus in associating with unbelievers.

Our research suggests that if Olivia had been sincerely concerned about the spiritual welfare of her new friends, if she had befriended the Low Riders in order to help them and not to share their lifestyle, her parents might have had some basis for optimism. However, the weight of evidence from Scripture, experience and our research proves that Olivia's movement into the bad crowd was spiritually perilous. Olivia's vulnerability rested not so much in the friendships she had formed as in her attitude toward the unbelieving crowd. Attitude, it turns out, makes all the difference.

Attitudes Toward Unbelieving Friends

Our research uncovered something quite fascinating. The most important issue is not whether a Christian teen has non-Christian friends. Friendship with an unbeliever may in fact have no negative consequences (that is, one may indeed be a "friend of sinners" as our Lord was). The crucial issue is, *With what attitude is the friendship viewed?* Does the Christian closely identify with the non-Christian? Is there "psychological closeness" between the Christian and non-Christian friend? If the answer is yes, then risk is involved. If no, the friendship is clearly less dangerous.

That the attitude about the friendship is as significant as the friendship itself becomes clear when we compare virginity rates to various attitudes toward friendships. For example, adolescents who say that their non-church friends sadden them experience higher virginity rates than teens who say that their non-church friends make them happy (77 percent vs. 69 percent). Apparently, Christian teens who can recognize and grieve over the problems of their non-Christian friends are less likely to imitate the mistakes of their unbelieving friends.

Virginity rates also differ depending on how closely Christian teens identify with their non-Christian friends' values. A very important concept to consider is "psychological distance." If the distance is great, then the Christian adolescent is less likely to succumb to non-Christian values. A virginity rate of 79 percent is found among those who feel "different from" their non-Christian friends, but a 64 percent virginity rate occurs among those who perceive themselves as "similar to" their worldly friends. In other words, if teens embrace the values of their non-Christian friends, one can expect lower rates of chastity; however, if teens maintain distance—moral, psychological and spiritual—rates of chastity are higher.

Those who feel low identificaton with non-church friends have a much higher rate of purity. In fact, the rate of virginity is twice as high among those who do not identify with the non-religious. This same pattern also was found in connection with intimate touching. Adolescents who identify closely with non-church members indicate a higher frequency of intimate touching. Conversely, there is a much better rate of abstaining from physical intimacy when a person does not feel an identification with worldly friends. A similar pattern occurred when we looked at pornography. Pornography avoidance was higher among teens who considered themselves "assertive" over their friends (67 percent) compared with those who report being influenced by friends (46 percent).

To summarize, teens who strongly identify with their non-religious friends are spiritually vulnerable.

They are inclined to lower their standards and adopt the norms of their non-believing peers. These teens are not simply living "in the world," a laudable Christian goal (John 17:11,18), but they have taken an ominous step beyond Christ's teaching by becoming one "of the world" (John 17:14-19). Olivia's parents failed to see this subtle but catastrophic difference in their heated discussion with their wayward daughter. Only time could reveal the spiritually devastating consequences of Olivia's close identification with her friends in the Low Riders. Paul was clearly on the mark when he said "Bad company corrupts good character" if the association means close identification with bad companions. But Jesus affirms a different principle when He calls us to be "the friend of sinners," assuming of course we do not adopt the values of the sinner.

Our study raises some important questions about how it is possible to be a friend to one in the world. How can one truly be a friend without also feeling close identification with the sinner? At this point we issue a major caution: Most adolescents find it almost impossible to be close friends with worldly peers without being overwhelmed by the secular standards of the peer group. The fact that this statement is so implies neither a weakness in the gospel nor necessarily a flaw in the Christian adolescent. It merely shows that only those who have a mature, developed sense of self can handle the relentless pressure of a contrary value system. Developmentally, most adolescents simply have not achieved that level of maturity. Yes, teens do need to "run with a group," but the crowd ought to espouse positive values. Otherwise, trouble is almost certain.

Hidden Motivations for Problem Friendships

Before we examine the decided benefits of strong Christian friendships, we need to discuss what prompts many teen-agers to form harmful relationships, which is a point that Olivia's parents needed very much to comprehend. Negative friendships often signify deeper problems, such as low self-esteem and feelings of powerlessness. Teens who seek out problem friends are not running to the group in order to be bad. They are choosing the group because they feel inadequate, and the group promises acceptance.

Often harmful friendships become part of a passive-aggressive strategy. When young people are angry but have no way to express their anger openly, they sometimes choose bad companions to declare indirectly the frustration that cannot be expressed openly. Incidentally, this principle helps explain other forms of negative behavior such as the practice of the occult. The occult is popular among many teens today because it promises power and a means of retaliation. For the passive-aggressive child of Christian parents, the occult offers the ultimate (and most devastating) power against mom and dad.

Negative friendships are usually symptoms of other unstated and often larger problems troubling the family. Parents are often unable to see or face these deeper problems, so they attack the symptom, the bad friends, rather than the core problem. Such parents who find themselves continually frustrated by futile discussions of friends would do well to listen to clinical psychologist Bob Sturgeon: "When parents fight with their kids about friends, they are in a battle they will never win." How futile to focus on friendships when serious hidden problems are being ignored! Such misdirected discussion is like fussing over a scratch when the person has a bleeding ulcer.

The tendency to misjudge the real problem is illustrated by a frustrated father who called his daughter's therapist to say, "I've had it with Becky. I'm tired of those kids she's running with. I'm fed up with her disobedience. God wants me to take charge of this family, so unless she changes her attitude and gives up those friends, I'm taking away the privilege of therapy. I've decided this is a battle I'm going to win." So he took Becky out of therapy, unaware that the real problem was not her friends, but his lack of acceptance of his daughter. The real disease, a very bad father-daughter relationship, loomed too large and too close for the father to see it. It was much easier to attack the symptom—Becky's friends. His "corrective" action greatly compounded his daughter's problems. Parents lose by "winning" in these maneuvers. A few months later, Becky was pregnant and permanently estranged from her father.

The Leaven of Good Friends

If harm may result from non-Christian friendships, is the opposite true? Do church friends lead to a higher morality? So it seems. A 78 percent virginity rate exists among those who identify with, and feel similar to, their church friends, which compares with a 56 percent virginity rate among those who feel very different from their church friends.

Virginity rates are noticeably higher when teens feel close identification with their church peers. On the other hand, if they feel remote from their Christian peers, virginity rates are lower.

- When church friends make teens happy, the virginity rate is 77 percent compared to 46 percent when their church friends make them sad.
- When church friends encourage them, there is a 77 percent virginity rate compared to 52 percent when their church friends are discouraging.
- When their church friends are "religious," there is a 75 percent virginity rate compared to 38 percent when their church friends are seen as "nonreligious."
- When being with church friends is important, the virginity rate is 79 percent compared to 63 percent when being with church friends is not important.

The same patterns occur when we look at issues like intimate touching and pornography. Identification with church friends, particularly those who are truly religiously committed, has an obvious positive effect on adolescent behavior.

Implications: Hot Dogs and Cold Water

A major conclusion from this research is the real value of youth and family programs. Effective ministries can and do foster healthy friendships, which in turn encourage moral behavior and long-term involvement in the church. Youth and family programs that build solid relationships are priceless. Unfortunately, not everyone understands this.

An enthusiastic young preacher hoped to initiate a number of activities to encourage the young people in his new congregation. In a business meeting of the congregation, he proposed a wiener roast for the youth group, pointing out all the good that could come from the fellowship. But one man declared, "If you start 'em off on hot dogs, you will have to keep feeding 'em hot dogs from now on." The committee agreed. They flatly rejected the poor minister's proposal.

What pained the minister most was the thought of little Sarah, a 14-year-old member who was becoming disillusioned with church. He wanted to do something to nourish her faith, even if it began with something as simple as a wiener roast. The minister was disheartened as he saw Sarah slipping away from the faith. When she was 18, she hastily married an unbeliever, and she abandoned the church altogether. Within months of her marriage, she visited the preacher and reported that her husband had led her into a very immoral way of life. Sarah was thoroughly disillusioned with life.

Reflecting on this incident 20 years later, the minister is convinced that if the church had had a strong youth program, Sarah might have been saved. Obviously, Sarah needed more than a wiener roast to keep her in the community of believers, but, simple as they are, such gatherings over time do solidify relationships that sustain teen-agers. Today, Sarah's minister laments that the church might have lost Sarah for the price of a hot dog.

To those church leaders who think it a waste of time to serve cookies and punch and who say, "We should be about the business of saving souls," we suggest that it takes both kinds of outreach. One activity actually may be an instrument of the other. The giving of a cup of cold water—or a cup of punch or a hot dog for that matter—is not a "secular" act at all when it is offered in Jesus' name. Those who depreciate fellowship activities need to re-examine their theology and harmonize it with Matthew's Gospel: "And if anyone gives a cup of cold water to one of these little ones because he is my disciple, I tell you the truth, he will certainly not lose his reward" (10:42; cf. 18:10-14; 25:31-46).

How can one develop genuine community, lasting ties of fellowship, in the absence of frequent sharing? It's impossible. In formulating the types of activities and in determining their frequency, certain questions must be answered, such as, Will the activities encourage growth in fellowship with God and with one another? Whatever is done, however mundane, must ultimately be part of some larger design to bring teens into fellowship with God. We must also ask, What will it take to keep our children constructively involved with one another? We must do whatever is necessary to keep our children together, help them enjoy one another's company, and learn interdependency.

Virtually every authority on today's adolescents points out their desperate longing for meaningful friendships. In *Reaching Out: The Three Movements of The Spiritual Life*, Henri Nouwen describes quite accurately the suffocating loneliness that plagues many of our teens today:

> Loneliness is one of the most universal sources of human suffering today. Psychiatrists and clinical psychologists speak about it as the most frequently expressed complaint and the root not only of an increasing number of suicides but also of alcoholism, drug use, different psychosomatic symptoms—such as headaches, stomach and low-back pains—and of a large number of traffic accidents. Children, adolescents, adults and old people are in growing degree exposed to the contagious disease of loneliness in a world in which a competitive individualism tries to reconcile itself with a culture that speaks about togetherness, unity and community as the ideals to strive for.[1]

Our teens who feel such forlornness are particularly vulnerable to anyone promising acceptance and understanding. The church must be in the business of helping teens find healthy, constructive relationships. If we help them find solid Christian friends, they are not necessarily "home free," but they are in a much better position to resist the temptations of a secular culture.

Our research confirms that healthy friendships do encourage ethical living. However, when adolescents closely identify with bad friends, trouble is certain.

Remember Olivia? Her parents yielded to Olivia's plea to let her choose her own friends, in this case the "Low Riders." Mother and Dad went against their better judgment, cut their daughter loose, and provided no guidance or monitoring at all. Even worse, the parents failed to look at the deeper family problems that prompted their daughter to seek out the rebel crowd in the first place. That was when Olivia was 15. A year later, she was addicted to crack and other drugs. At 16, Olivia was in a psychiatric hospital with a serious drug and alcohol problem. Proper teaching about friendship, an aggressive youth outreach, and vigilant and responsive parents could have saved Olivia.

Our Mission: In the World, Not of the World

Our mission is multiple. First, we must begin to look at our families holistically. We must see beyond the particular problems in adolescent friendships in order to discern the underlying forces prompting some children to establish problem friendships. Simone Weil is correct when she says, "Love sees what is invisible." We are called to see broadly and deeply, to see the invisible, in other words.

Second, we must testify that friendship is truly an issue of *theological* significance about which the Bible has much to say. Understanding the dynamics of good friendship is not just good sociology. Friendship is a basic theological issue, an implicit expression of God's relationship with man. Abraham, the archetype of the true believer, was called "the friend of God." Jesus called His disciples "friends." Knowing how to be a good friend in an earthly context, knowing how to develop close attachments to believers, and knowing how to form redemptive ties with unbelievers are fundamental Christian objectives that deserve much more attention in our preaching and teaching.

Human friendship is actually a symbol of the very relationship that God seeks with mankind. This is the thought behind Thomas Browne's insightful observation, "I have loved my friend as I do virtue, my soul, my God. From hence methinks I do conceive how God loves man, what happiness there is in the love of God."[2] Indeed, a good friendship (like a good marriage) is a kind of laboratory for understanding the divine-human relationship. Christians should be the world's authorities on true friendship.

Finally, we need much more instruction about how to practice friendship in its various forms. Parents and teachers should help adolescents develop interpersonal skills, which include active listening, greetings, cooperation, conflict management, and assertiveness. These skills are vehicles to loving our fellow humans. The love of our neighbors is one of the two basic commands given by our Lord. How do we move beyond superficial relationships to redemptive ones? How do we practice friendship toward "sinners"? Toward those who are not like us? Toward the dangerous people who do not know God? Can the Christian embrace all people in the name of Christ? How is this possible?

In short, we need a theology of friendship, grounded in Scripture, leading to practical insights in how to be friends *in* the world without being friends *of* the world.

Endnotes

1. Henri Nouwen, *Reaching Out: The Three Movements of the Spiritual Life* (New York: Doubleday, 1975), 15.
2. Thomas Browne, *The Major Works*, ed. C. A. Patrides (London: Penguin, 1977), 143.

CHAPTER 6

CONGREGATIONAL STYLES AND SEXUALITY

"So too, at the present time there is a remnant chosen by grace. And if by grace, then it is no longer by works; if it were, grace would no longer be grace" (Romans 11:5,6).

"The quality of mercy is not strained;
It droppeth as the gentle rain from heaven
Upon the place beneath. It is twice blest;
It blesseth him that gives and him that takes . . .
It is an attribute to God Himself,
And earthly power doth then show likest God's
When mercy seasons justice."
—William Shakespeare

Everyone knows that churches, like people and families, have distinct personalities. Each congregation has its own style, approach and atmosphere even if it subscribes to the same general beliefs of other congregations. Visit two different congregations in the same town, and it is quickly obvious that congregations, like people, have unique personalities.

Peters and Waterman, in their best-selling work *In Search of Excellence,* have shown how a group can be viewed as an "organizational culture." A congregation is also an "organizational culture," championing certain themes that undergird the group and shape its members. Because this statement is true, it is important to consider what kind of congregational style young people are used to when we discuss their sexual behavior. Some researchers have studied the effect of variables like church attendance and personal faith on adolescent behavior, but we are not aware of a single study describing the role of congregational styles on adolescent sexual behavior. This matter deserves our closest attention.

In our preliminary research we administered some pilot tests, asking adolescents about the "personality" of their congregations. The results were so striking that we decided to devote a major section of our questionnaire to items that would enable us to identify congregational traits that could then be correlated with sexual attitudes and behavior. Our respondents measured their congregations according to five different scales:

- Overly strict vs. permissive
- Legalistic vs. grace-oriented
- Holds grudges vs. forgiving
- Out-of-touch vs. relevant
- Insensitive vs. sensitive

The responses to the survey introduce some momentous issues. Although our study is intended to be sociological, we cannot ignore the theological implications of this information. For centuries Christians have debated questions of grace and law, for example. Our research suggests that such theological debates are not merely theoretical. Once a particular doctrinal stance permeates a congregation, it shapes the personality of the fellowship. These particular beliefs and attitudes, in turn, color the thinking and sexual behavior of the teen-agers. In other words, what the local church thinks and believes collectively affects how its young people behave—in some surprising ways.

Strict vs. Permissive Churches

Would teens from "permissive" churches be more inclined to be sexually permissive compared to the children from strict churches? It seems logical enough, but the facts don't back up that theory. Teens from overly strict churches fared no better than those from permissive churches. Adolescents were most likely to be sexually lax if they came from either end of the spectrum—from either overly permissive or overly strict congregations. The highest rate of virginity, one must note as well, is found in churches that have achieved a balance between permissiveness and strictness (72 percent virginity from "balanced" systems vs. 57 percent from the overly strict churches).

One might suppose that teen-agers belonging to a grace-oriented church might be more sexually active, but our data suggest just the opposite. The fact is, overly strict congregations produce teen-agers more inclined to act out sexual behavior. We are certainly not suggesting that an overly permissive congregation is better; however, we must conclude that an extremely rigid environment does not necessarily inspire moral behavior. Our research in fact confirms Paul's instruction to the Colossians: "Forced piety" and "self-mortification" are of "no use at all in combatting sensuality" (2:23 NEB).

In overly rigid congregations, a sharp sense of right and wrong may be proclaimed, but the spirit of encouragement and the motivation to ethical living are often in short supply. This point is illustrated by Stephanie, an 18-year-old who, during the invitation hymn one Sunday morning, walked down the aisle with tears flowing down her cheeks. She sat on the front pew and wrote that she had been sexually immoral and wanted the forgiveness of God and the congregation. After her confession was read, several members gave her the hugs and affirmation she needed, indicating their forgiveness. However, one church leader came up to her and declared in a brusque tone: "Well, young lady, I guess you will learn to say no next time, won't you?" While his words barely said, "I forgive you," his attitude proclaimed, "You are not forgiven."

In congregations where rules override concern for people, where Sabbath-keeping and the showbread are more important than human needs, our kids seem to find it more difficult to live morally pure lives. A life governed by negatives such as, "Do not handle! Do not taste! Do not touch!" lacks power to restrain sensual indulgence, Paul teaches (Colossians 2:21,22). Our research helps explain why this is so.

Legalism and Grace

For centuries Christians have struggled with the dichotomy of grace and law. Does believing in grace, for example, encourage sexual laxity? Some Christians fear an emphasis upon grace, supposing it will lead to "easy-believism," a casual attitude about rules, or even moral anarchy. At least in regard to our adolescents, such fears are unfounded. Sin doesn't necessarily increase because grace abounds.

If anything, an atmosphere of grace encourages self-restraint and moderation. Of our respondents from grace-oriented churches, 73 percent are virgins compared with 64 percent from legalistic churches. Furthermore, when we examine pornography rates, we find that adolescents from legalistic churches use pornography far more than youths from the "grace" churches. Specifically, 61 percent of our respondents from grace churches avoid pornography, compared to 47 percent from legalistic churches. Consider the additional comparisons listed below:

- Of those who come from grace-oriented churches, 61 percent attempt to be consistent with Scripture, but only 45 percent of those from legalistic churches attempt to be consistent with Scripture.
- Six percent of the adolescents from grace-oriented churches tend to reject parental values, but 20 percent of those from legalistic churches reject parental values.
- Only 3 percent of youths from grace-oriented churches indicate that they intend to be sexually permissive on dates, but 8 percent of the respondents from legalistic churches say they have such intentions.

Uniformly, a difference between the youths of these two congregational styles is evident. The evidence strongly suggests that legalism, at least as it is perceived by adolescents, alienates them from parental and biblical values, leading to a greater incidence of immoral behavior.

Forgiving Churches

A central theme of the New Testament is forgiveness. Jesus taught His disciples to pray: "Forgive us our debts, as we also have forgiven our debtors" (Matthew 6:12). Peter was taught to forgive his brother seventy times seven. The questions arise: What happens to a young person who matures in an atmosphere in which the quality of mercy is often demonstrated? On the other hand, what happens to the young person who sees the opposite frequently—harshness, ill will and grudges? Does the fruit of the Spirit, or the absence of such fruit, have any effect on our teens? Yes, indeed. For example, 77 percent of our respondents from "forgiving" churches are virgins, but only 56 percent were virgins from "grudge-holding" churches.

When we talk about grudge-holding or forgiving churches, of course we do not mean to suggest labels that characterize every member of the body. Every congregation is a mix of people, some critical and censuring, others tolerant and forbearing. But in creating these categories, we are reflecting what social scientists have taught us about group behavior, namely, that groups do have distinctive personalities. Though a social group (such as a church) is a company of individuals, nonetheless, collectively, a group personality emerges. Just as some people are rigid and unforgiving, so are some congregations, collectively speaking. By contrast, other congregations are generally more tolerant and accepting.

Our research shows that adolescents do better in an affirming, forgiving atmosphere, which says in effect, "Because no one is without sin, we have no right to cast stones."

The forgiveness imperative is precisely what affected Jan so dramatically. Jan is a college freshman who recounts a life-changing incident in her local church four years ago. As a ninth grader, she thought a lot about sex. Then something happened to her best friend, Beth, an event not soon to be forgotten.

One Sunday morning Jan witnessed Beth and her entire family respond to the minister's invitation. Beth's dad was the first to speak. His remarks before the whole church were addressed to Beth. "For as long as your mom and I remember, we prayed for a daughter like you. God answered our prayer—you were born!" He then spoke of the love and appreciation he and his wife had for their daughter and of their commitment to stay by her in what they were about to reveal as a family crisis. Then Beth spoke, telling of her own pain. She was pregnant out of wedlock. Beth's brother also spoke and affirmed how much he cared for Beth. Then Jan remembers Beth's standing before the church, asking forgiveness. All the members responded by leaving their seats and surrounding the family. The whole church expressed its love and forgiveness, weeping with the family for half an hour or more.

Four years later, Jan vividly recalls this incident. This confession of wrong followed by communal forgiveness made such an impression on her that it has greatly influenced her to remain pure despite several tempting circumstances in later years. The church's forgiving nature was an incentive for Jan to remain chaste.

Relevant Churches

A "relevant" church in this study refers to one that teen-agers consider to be signficant to their lives. Being relevant is not being "trendy," but it does mean being a church whose teaching and ministries "make sense." The activities are appropriate to the interests and understandings of adolescents. Although one may decry the shallow call for relevance that often characterized the rebellious '60s (which was often just a call for selfish indulgence), there is a higher kind of relevance about which churches ought to be concerned, a relevance that includes dealing with the issues of life honestly, being concerned and truthful about the problems of the human condition. Relevance in this sense, which includes a commitment to honest realism, has always characterized biblical Christianity.

Not surprisingly, adolescents from relevant churches have a different moral outlook and lifestyle from those from churches viewed as irrelevant, as Table 6.1 shows. In several significant ways, teens function better if they belong to churches viewed as relevant.

TABLE 6.1

	Relevant Churches	Irrelevant Churches
Virginity rate	77%	57%
Never resort to intimate touching	29%	17%
Identify with family values	25%	12%
High parental influence	41%	26%

Recently, a Christian physician in a small town told the youth minister in his church, "We really need some teaching in our congregation on sexuality from a biblical point of view." Agreeing with the doctor, the youth minister asked the elders to approve a four-week course of study on sexuality from a Christian perspective. The elders said no. Such a class has no place in the congregation, they said. Furthermore, they emphatically insisted that sexual questions were not an issue for the young people of their church. In fact, the class was partly rejected because it was too relevant. The youth minister and the local physician were aware that the daughter of one of the elders had recently had an abortion. Irrelevancy, in this matter, borders on dishonesty—a flat refusal to come to terms with life, human nature, and the biblical mandate to give our children the instruction necessary to cope in the world.

Fortunately, other church leaders respond more positively to the sexual crisis. When a group of 30 families decided to leave a congregation of about 300 people, the elders were disturbed enough to find out why and to take action. The families' unhappiness stemmed from strong feelings that their children were not being attended to. Apparently, no malicious intent was intended in the neglect. The church's leaders simply had failed to see what was happening. They had failed to discern the considerable gap between routine congregational activities and the special problems their teens were facing. However, when they learned that these families felt unnurtured and spiritually adrift, these very leaders asked forgiveness for being out of touch. Within three months they established a dynamic new program to minister to families in the congregation and the community. The results of that family ministry have been so dramatic that the family ministry program is now recognized as one of the model programs in the United States.

The church in our day is undergoing a crisis of identity as it faces the 21st century. If our teens are unimpressed, if their emotional and spiritual hungerings are not fulfilled, and if they are disillusioned by our timid refusal to deal honestly with the real issues, then they will not be with us for long. We must respond to our youth in order to save them. We also need to respond to them in order to save ourselves. Our past refusal to face the problems of adolescent sexuality may, in fact, be rooted in a larger failure of our integrity. We may be in collective denial about many issues, of which the sexual issue is only one.

Sensitive Churches

Seventeen-year-old Amy responded to the invitation hymn one day at church, along with a number of others. The preacher had been rather long-winded that day, and it was getting late. He was obviously in a hurry when he took up the response cards. All who had answered the gospel invitation had written messages on their response cards, but Amy had taken unusual care to explain her reason for responding. She confessed that she had been sexually involved. She wanted to confess that specific sin, and she wanted the forgiveness of her brothers and sisters. She also wanted everyone to know the nature of her mistake so that others could learn from her error.

The preacher, on the spot, determined that that kind of information did not need to be shared with young and tender hearts, so he took it upon himself not to read Amy's specific request. He made very general comments about Amy, passing over her sin, her request, and her needs. That was when Amy was 17. Now 19, she no longer is a member of that congregation, but she is raising her baby by herself, a baby born out of wedlock. When she came forward at 17, she was not pregnant, but now, two years later, she recalls bitterly the lack of sensitivity of that congregation and of the preacher in particular, as she faces a difficult world as a single parent.

Christians are people of sensitivity. Jesus "knew what was in man." The touch of a single person in a huge crowd could alert Him to a spiritual need. He observed, listened, weighed, and then acted accordingly. Christ calls us to a similar kind of quick-eyed attentiveness. When our churches are characterized by this quality of discernment, wonderful things happen. "Sensitive" churches have significantly higher virginity rates than do "insensitive" churches. Specifically, 76 percent from the sensitive churches are virgins compared to 53 percent from insensitive churches. A sensitive fellowship can have a very powerful influence on adolescent behavior.

Conclusions: The Quality of Mercy

If the ambiance of the local church truly has serious effects on the lives of its teen-agers, then we must get serious about obtaining an accurate self-portrait. And, if we do not like what we see, we must correct the situation. We should be especially concerned about the dangers of over-control.

We are not advocating some kind of lawless fellowship, operating without boundaries. On the other hand, rigidity without loving flexibility will be seen as cruel and ruthless. It will alienate adolescents (and adults too, for that matter), and it may drive them to despair. The issue is not standards or rules, which we must have. The issue is whether we couch the rules in a system of grace and Christlike kindness that encourages moral behavior rather than discourages it. One may think of Hester Prynne, Nathaniel Hawthorne's famous figure who wore the scarlet letter. How much better she might have fared in a less puritanical community, one that tempered law with grace. Balance is the key.

Another important aspect is relevant to this issue of grace. Not only are we saved from past sin by grace, but our study suggests that grace also saves families from future pain. As with Beth in our earlier story, watching the operations of a grace-filled church can have wholesome, salutary effects on members who may be tempted later, even years later.

We may conclude that the spirit of forgiveness need not be feared because it makes a church "soft" or indifferent to moral standards. Quite the contrary, moral standards may be maintained more easily in an atmosphere of grace.

Finally, we are reminded that Jesus' church is eternally "relevant," not in the sense that the church is enslaved to daily trends and the whimsical fashions of an ever-changing society. Instead, like its Founder, the church lays down its life for people. The church is forever concerned about men's and women's deepest longings for spiritual sustenance. Like Jesus, the church meets people where they are in order to lead them where they need to be. It has an honest and realistic appreciation for the human condition. Its commitment to truth is fully consonant with its desire to be "relevant." God's people can be, must be, relevant in biblical ways. "Biblical ways" means understanding people's hurts, their weaknesses and their temptations and finding ways to lead them to God's teaching, requirements and holiness—though always with compassion. If we fail to do this, if we don't have one foot planted firmly in the world of Scripture and the other planted firmly in the world of contemporary men and women, we will be necessarily out of touch.

From this data about church styles we see clearly that we have an important mission before us. Church leaders, ministers and parents should begin with an honest inventory of how they perceive themselves, followed with a careful inquiry into their adolescents' perception of the local fellowship. Some church leaders may be disappointed to see how they are perceived; perhaps others will be pleasantly surprised. But the issue isn't how we view ourselves. The question is how adolescents view the congregation where they worship. The competing views must then be carefully weighed. The gaps may be large, but until we know where the chasm lies, we cannot build a bridge to the hearts of our young.

Once church leaders have an accurate understanding of their teens' view of the church, some sort of action will likely be necessary. Even minor shifts in meeting arrangements, in opportunities for service, and in worship procedures (such as including hymns that are especially meaningful to teens), can make a big difference in those perceptions. Some congregations may need to rethink more fundamental issues, such as their view of grace and law, forgiveness and discipline, and even the character and mission of Christianity itself. Such self-examination may be painful at times, but it could also mean becoming a healthier and more viable fellowship. Honest self-examination could even mean the difference between congregational demise or survival into the next century.

CHAPTER 7

DOES THE COMMUNITY OF FAITH MAKE A DIFFERENCE?

"But if we walk in the light, as he is in the light, we have fellowship with one another, and the blood of Jesus, his Son, purifies us from every sin" (1 John 1:7).

"The pious fellowship permits no one to be a sinner. So everybody must conceal his sin from himself and from the fellowship. We dare not be sinners. Many Christians are unthinkably horrified when a real sinner is suddenly discovered among the righteous. So we remain alone with our sin, living in lies and hypocrisy. The fact is that we are sinners!" —Dietrich Bonhoeffer, Life Together

---

Garrison Keillor tells a moving story of his high-school days in mythical Lake Wobegon. It seems that Mr. Detman, the principal, was worried that the pupils who lived in the country might get caught in a winter storm: "a blizzard would sweep in and the school buses be marooned on the roads and the children perish." Mr. Detman resolved his "winter fear" by assigning every farm kid to a house in town. In the event of a blizzard, each child would go to his "storm home."

In fact, no blizzard ever struck during school hours, yet the knowledge that he had a "storm home," a place of safety, nourished the boy's heart. Keillor's story becomes a parable of everyone's need for a place of spiritual and psychological safety. He writes in *Lake Wobegon Days:*

> No blizzard came during school hours that year, all the snowstorms were convenient evening or weekend ones, and I never got to stay with the Kloeckls [his assigned family], but they were often in my thoughts and they grew large in my imagination. My Storm Home. Blizzards aren't the only storms and not the worst by any means. I could imagine worse things. If the worst should come, I could go to the Kloeckls and knock on their door. "Hello," I'd say. "I'm your storm child."[1]

Ideally, the church is every Christian's "storm home." In the church God's "afflicted people will find refuge" (Isaiah 14:32). Christian teen-agers especially need a shelter from the continual hail of temptations and the blizzard of erotic messages.

Is the church today, we must ask, fulfilling this God-ordained mission of being "a refuge from the storm" (Isaiah 32:2)? Specifically, how much does the church help its teen-agers in their sexual struggles? Does the church really make a difference?

Surprisingly, these questions have seldom been faced squarely. If we are honest, we must admit that our reluctance to inquire stems from our fear of what we may learn. Perhaps our deepest anxiety is that Christian ministry may be ineffectual in the complex arena of teen-age sexuality. Many believe that this is precisely the case. A number of ministers have privately expressed their opinion that the church is having little effect on the way our teens exercise their sexuality. In effect they are saying that our "storm children" have adapted themselves to ways of a rather cold world. Are they correct?

Recently in a high-school Bible class, while a youth minister was teaching a lesson on the importance of maintaining one's sexual purity, a 16-year-old varsity cheerleader responded, "What you say may be true, but if you're looking for a virgin in our high school, good luck!" It doesn't take many encounters like this one before you begin to wonder if our teens have accommodated themselves to the realities of a post-Christian culture.

Yet we must be careful not to base our judgment of teens on such haphazard testimony. A great need exists for a more comprehensive and balanced view so that the church may effectively minister in this critical area. We have attempted to shed some light on the subject by examining five distinct areas of church life—youth ministry, Bible classes, preaching, church attendance and church leadership. We have examined each of these areas to find out what impact (if any) these dimensions of church life are having on adolescent sexuality. What we learned should be helpful and even occasionally heartening. For many of our children, the church is serving well as a refuge and a haven from the storms generated by the sexual revolution.

YOUTH MINISTRY

For many years lingering doubts have existed about the efficacy of youth ministry programs. Some critics claim that youth programs are only passing fashions that will soon join the heap of outmoded ecclesiastical fads. We disagree. One unexpected discovery in our research is the solid evidence that youth and family ministries do make a significant contribution to the moral and spiritual development of teen-agers. Over half of our respondents (54 percent) find youth ministries "very" or "somewhat" helpful. A minority (46 percent) reports youth ministry as "occasionally" or "not at all" helpful.

One important finding concerns the relationship between virginity rates and attitudes towards youth ministry. Adolescents who consider youth ministry extremely helpful have an 80 percent virginity rate compared to a 58 percent rate among adolescents who consider youth ministry unhelpful.

As we have noted earlier, technical virginity or intimate touching is a serious problem among today's teens. We, therefore, asked the teens to tell us if they ever resorted to intimate touching, and we compared their responses to their attitude toward youth ministry. Adolescents who claim to have been helped by youth ministry are two and one-half times more likely to refrain from this kind of behavior. Only 15 percent of those helped by youth ministry engage in intimate touching, while 38 percent of those feeling negatively toward youth ministry engage in intimate touching. Similarly, adolescents who find youth ministry "relevant" are twice as likely to refrain from oral sex.

Because the Bible is a primary resource for coping with moral problems, including sexual temptation, we wanted to know what impact youth ministry may have upon a young person's desire to know and follow Scripture. One question concerns teen-agers' "consistency with Scripture." We asked: "To what degree do you attempt to make your sexual attitudes and behavior consistent with the Bible?" We discovered that those adolescents who find youth ministry helpful report twice as much "consistency with Scripture" as those who devalue youth ministry (30 percent vs. 16 percent).

Sometimes parents question the value of youth ministries because they think involvement in youth programs diminishes parental control. For this reason, we asked about the relationship between youth ministry and parental influence. Significantly, those who find youth ministry helpful also identify positively with parental values, but those who feel negatively toward youth ministry identify less with parental values (25 percent vs. 15 percent). Fears about loss of parental influence prove to be unfounded.

Our research indicates that youth ministry programs are making an important contribution to the spiritual life of teen-agers. The New Testament call to live a transformed life is more likely and more possible when a strong youth or family ministry program is operating within the local congregation.

Attendance at Youth Activities

As never before in history, parents and teen-agers feel pressure to participate in an exhausting list of activities almost every day. Parents and children literally run between play practice and soccer, gymnastics and piano lessons, Scouts and pep rallies, fund-raisers and football games. Parents and children alike are suffering from activity overload. In all this frenzy, where exactly do congregational youth activities belong? In many churches, youth activities must compete vigorously with a smorgasbord of exciting secular choices. In the crunch, some parents frankly wonder about the importance of congregational youth activities.

How important is it that our teens be active participants in church activities? To find out, we statistically correlated attendance at youth activities and worship with sexual behavior. The results are enlightening. Of those who attend youth activities all the time, 86 percent are virgins compared with only 46 percent who never attend youth activities. This gap of 40 percent between the highest and lowest attenders confirms the need to choose wisely among competing programs, to resist activity overload, and to keep young people involved in church programs.

Next we examined attendance at youth activities as it relates to technical virginity. Of those who attend all youth activities, 36 percent avoid intimate touching. However, among non-attenders at youth activities, only 10 percent never engage in intimate touching. This 26 percent difference underscores the fact that sexual behavior is closely related to participation in church programs.

Because previous research has indicated that beliefs and actual behavior are highly correlated, we recognized the need to measure attendance at youth activities against the item on the test called "intentions" (i.e., how far the adolescent intended to go on a date). When we assessed the category of "intentions to engage in sexual intercourse," we found that attendance at youth activities makes an important difference. Specifically, less than 2 percent of those who attend youth activities intend to engage in sexual intercourse on a date; however, of those who never attend youth activities, 12 percent intend to engage in sex on a date.

We were also curious about attendance at youth activities as it relates to pornography usage: 64 percent of those who attend all youth activities never use pornography, but among non- or low-attenders only 41 percent never use pornography. Apparently, adolescents involved in youth ministry turn to pornography far less than other teens.

Some church leaders and parents have feared that youth programs may subvert parental values by detaching teens from the home environment. This belief is emphatically not the case according to our research.

In fact, involvement in youth programs is positively linked with parental influence. Only 16 percent of those who never attend youth activities say they are influenced by their parents, but 45 percent of those who attend regularly say their parents are an important influence in their lives. In other words, frequent attendance at youth activities strengthens the adolescent perspective on the importance of listening to parents. Attendance at youth activities is also a predictor of a young person's acceptance of parental values. Of those adolescents who attend youth activities all the time, 28 percent identify with parental values compared with only 9 percent who never attend.

To summarize, this national profile of teens presents an exceptionally consistent picture. We now know that attendance at youth activities does make a difference in such areas as virginity, pornography, promiscuous intentions when on a date, consistency with Scripture, and identification with parental values.

Church leaders sometimes are tempted to curtail youth ministry programs in order to balance the church budget, but the evidence shows that this ministry is a poor place to try to save a few dollars. Youth programs serve a vital function by supporting and complementing family values.

BIBLE CLASSES

When our children reach the teen years, we sometimes have difficulty in persuading them to see the importance of Bible classes. "It's boring," they sometimes say. We can easily find fault with the teacher, the curriculum, and the other members in the class. And so parents may be tempted to yield to pressure during these critical years. When parents feel the intense competition between the big school event and church attendance, between the club social or the church retreat, what are they to do? Our research suggests that children need involvement in church, especially in the adolescent years.

We asked teens to indicate if their Bible classes helped them deal with sexual issues, and we compared their responses to a variety of factors. We discovered that those adolescents who found Bible class helpful had a 77 percent virginity rate compared to only 55 percent among those who did not value Bible classes. Among those who found Bible classes relevant to their sexual problems, 33 percent said they never participated in intimate touching compared to 16 percent among those who devalued Bible class. We found a comparable correlation in the area of pornography usage. Of the teens who highly value Bible classes, 58 percent said they never looked at pornography; however, of the teens who find Bible classes unhelpful, 46 percent said they never resorted to pornography.

Bible class attitudes also were compared with the attempt to live consistently with Scripture. Adolescents who find Bible classes extremely helpful had a 24 percent rate of consistency with Scripture compared to only 10 percent among those who judged Bible classes unhelpful.

We also thought it important to see if Bible class attitudes had anything to do with sexual intentions on a date. The difference is modest but important between teens who value Bible classes and those who do not. Of those who believe Bible classes are effective in helping teens with sexual problems, only 2 percent showed permissive intentions on a date. This figure rises to 7 percent among those who view Bible classes in a poor light.

Finally, wanting to know if Bible classes support parental values, we compared "attitude with Bible classes" and acceptance of parental values and parental influence. The evidence argues strongly for the power of Bible classes to advance parental values. For example, of those who find Bible classes helpful, 27 percent agreed with parental values, but among those who consider Bible classes unhelpful, only 12 percent shared parental values.

In our moments of discouragement when we fear that our teens are finding the Bible unimportant and beside the point, we ought to recall this evidence. Teens who are not participants in an array of church experiences, of which youth ministry and Bible classes are a part, are certainly at spiritual risk. Of course, no perfect shelter from today's secular society can be found. The youth minister, the Bible class teacher, and the minister cannot guarantee the safety and protection of our youth. The church is not a charm or good luck piece that wards off evil magically; temptation is inescapable. On the other hand, our study shows that the church does provide a place of safety in the storm. Spiritual survival is greatly enhanced when young adults make the church their "storm home."

THE ROLE OF PREACHING

Adolescents sometimes leave the distinct impression that they would rather do anything than listen to a sermon. Many ministers despair over breaking through the seemingly impenetrable wall that looms between them and the "youth culture." Their frustration is compounded by the often repeated claim that half our young people eventually leave the church. Is today's preacher called to a task far beyond his ability or talent? Is he a kind of Don Quixote, foolishly contending with secular windmills?

Before yielding to despair, ministers should recall that adolescents often mask their real feelings. What seems apparent is often misleading. This point is particularly true when considering adolescents' attitudes toward preaching and the impact of preaching on teen behavior. Surprising as it may be, many Christian teens value preaching and are changed by it.

Attitudes toward preaching are closely related to sexual behavior in several ways. Of those who find preaching helpful with sexual struggles, 70 percent are virgins; but only 60 percent are virgins among those who find preaching unhelpful. Adolescents who view preaching as helpful are almost twice as likely to avoid intimate touching. We also find that young people who regard preaching positively use pornography less (62 percent vs. 50 percent).

Do attitudes toward preaching have anything to do with an adolescent's desire to live consistently with Scripture? Most definitely. Among those adolescents who find preaching helpful, there is a 32 percent rate of consistency compared to only an 8 percent consistency rate among those who say preaching is unhelpful. We may conclude that preachers who faithfully relate the Bible message to real problems in the lives of teens can expect to help their teen-age listeners to live harmoniously with God's will.

Attitudes toward preaching are also closely related to young people's evaluations of their parents. For instance, 51 percent of those who appreciate preaching also say they accept parental influence, and 29 percent of them also accept their parents' values. By contrast, of those who regard preaching unfavorably, only 11 percent accept parental values.

Preaching also correlates to intentions on a date. Less than 1 percent of those who found preaching effective in dealing with sexual matters indicate any intentions to be permissive on a date, but among those who minimize preaching, 10 percent have intentions to be sexually permissive on a date.

CHURCH ATTENDANCE

Of course preaching cannot be separated from church attendance. When church attendance is correlated with virginity rates, we see that those who attend frequently are much less sexually active than occasional attenders. As attendance falls, so do virginity rates, dramatically so:

Virginity Rate	Frequency of Attendance
81%	3 times weekly (or more)
63%	2 times weekly
51%	2 or 3 times per month
36%	Once a month
28%	Rarely attend

We cannot promise that sitting on a church pew will keep young people virgins, but the evidence shows a decisive link between church attendance and virginity.

Because counselors and therapists are saying that increasing numbers of teen-agers are practicing various forms of intimate touching, we were concerned to learn whether or not church attendance has any bearing on this practice. Although the findings are not as dramatic, we do find that churchgoing does relate to the issue. Among adolescents who attend church three or more times each week, 30 percent avoid intimate touching, compared with only 12 percent among those who rarely or never attend.

Church attendance affects other areas as well: pornography usage and sexual intentions on a date, for example. Young people who attend church often (three or more meetings weekly) tend to avoid pornography much more than those who rarely attend (62 percent vs. 38 percent). Intentions to be sexually permissive on a date increase as church attendance drops: 2 percent of those who attend church often intend to be sexually permissive compared with 14 percent of those who rarely attend church. Apparently, participation in the life of a local church is related to moral integrity.

When we compare church attendance to parental influence and values, we find the same patterns as in other areas. Church attendance has a positive influence: 43 percent of those who attend church activities three times or more weekly accept strong parental influence compared with only 16 percent of those who rarely attend.

Bringing our children to church is one thing, but their *wanting* to be there is quite another. It seems important, therefore, to measure teen-agers' personal desire to be present in church services. Most teen-agers want to be in church (72 percent); less than a third preferred not to attend (28 percent). In summary, a positive attitude toward the assembly reveals the same patterns we have been describing throughout this chapter. A positive attitude toward the Christian assembly, coupled with faithful attendance, is indispensible to developing the moral self.

CHURCH LEADERS

As we weigh the church's contribution to the spiritual and moral growth of its young, we must examine the role of the church's spiritual leaders, its elders or shepherds. Consider the feelings of Joan, a deeply distressed, newly divorced mother:

> Everywhere I turn at church my kids and I are ignored. I don't think anyone here cares about what we are going through. Not one elder has asked me how I am doing, and many of the church leaders seem to be more concerned about budgets than people. They think more about the building and the parking lot than about my problems. Now I find out that my daughter is pregnant. Do you really think they are going to care?

Joan's comments illustrate the concern of many church members when a crisis descends on them. They really expect, and long for, compassionate shepherds to come to their aid. Fortunately, many church leaders do care, and they take pains to minister to families like Joan's.

However, much work is still to be done, especially in bringing the pastoral concern and wisdom of elders into the lives of adolescents. In many congregations an unfortunate chasm separates the shepherds and the adolescent flock. In such churches, the teen-agers do not perceive church leaders as being very helpful in their struggle with sexual problems.

Unlike the three previous findings (concerning Bible classes, preaching and church attendance), the majority of respondents do not find the church's elders to be helpful. Broadly speaking, two distinct groups appear: those who find elders helpful in dealing with sexual struggles (44 percent) and those who do not (56 percent).

When we examine virginity rates, the practice of intimate touching, consistency with Scripture, and acceptance of parental values, we see that attitudes about elders make a modest difference. Among adolescents who find elders a valuable resource, there is a 77 percent virginity rate compared to a 67 percent rate among those who find elders unhelpful. Comparable findings may be seen in the practice of intimate touching (29 percent vs. 21 percent). Similarly, adolescents who value elderships were more consistent with Scripture (22 percent) compared to those who do not esteem elders (13 percent). Of those who find elders helpful, 27 percent accept parental values, compared with 13 percent of those who minimize the value of elders.

Although the trends are moderate, they reinforce the general conclusion that church leadership, like youth ministry, Bible school, and preaching, do contribute to positive adolescent behavior.

However, the contribution of shepherds to adolescent spirituality should be greater than it is. The institutional nature of today's elderships seems to remove the shepherds from the daily life of teen-agers. Most elders are not near at hand as far as adolescents are concerned. This distance is regrettable because it deprives teen-agers of the most mature spiritual resources within the community of faith. Certainly a goal of church leaders today should be to bridge the gap, to know all their sheep, and to give encouragement to their adolescent members.

Conclusions: Ministries and Morality

From this data we may safely argue that preachers, youth ministers, and church leaders do contribute to the spiritual and moral development of teens. The good news is that parents are not alone in trying to help their children struggle with sexual temptation. Though far from perfect, the community of faith is a spiritual haven. The family of God is alive, functioning reasonably well, and motivating young Christians to live pure lives in a world hostile to spiritual values.

When adolescents esteem youth programs, Bible classes, preaching, and church leaders (and 60 percent do), for the most part they respond with chaste behavior. On the other hand, the sobering note is that when youth discount these ministries (as 40 percent do), less moral restraint is practiced.

We must value all ministries that help adolescents face the difficult circumstances of growing up in the storms of a secular culture. Because our youth are assaulted by sexual messages every day and in almost every waking moment of their lives, the church has no time for petty competition between ministries. We need a variety of church programs as bold and daring as the stakes are momentous.

Yet we must understand that not all youth programs or church ministries are created equal. Not all programs are equally successful. We are calling for ministries of a certain type, ones that recognize the real struggles and needs of youth, ones that provide

123

truly spiritual resources, and ones that have the courage to address all the issues boldly.

In order to establish ministries like these, we must have the right kind of people to inspire, to build, and to direct them. We need committed parents, ministers, and church leaders who are unafraid to confront the real problems facing our youth, confidently proclaiming that God's Word holds the answers even in this difficult area of life.

Garrison Keillor imagines a conversation with his "storm parents" in his account of the "storm child." One of them says, "Terrible storm. They say it's going to get worse before it stops. I just pray for anyone who's out in this."[2]

In a way, Keillor has summarized Christian ministry to adolescents at the end of our century. Our children stand at the door in the cold. "Hello," they say, "I'm your storm child." The storm is terrible, and it's going to get worse before it gets better. What are we to do? Surely our mission is to draw these children in from the bitter cold and to nourish their souls. We are called to pray for them, love them, and minister to them. In short, as the community of faith, we must resolve to be a better storm home for our children.

Endnotes

1. Garrison Keillor, *Lake Wobegon Days* (New York: Viking Press, 1985), 249.
2. *Ibid.*

CHAPTER
8

THE END OF INNOCENCE: MEDIA AND SEXUALITY

"The holy tube shines upon us implacably, greedily, a secular god of sorts, determined in its own manner to exert its sway over our hearts, if not our minds . . ."—Robert Coles

"And now, my friends, all that is true, all that is noble, all that is just and pure, all that is lovable and gracious, whatever is excellent and admirable—fill all your thoughts with these things" (Philippians 4:8 NEB).

"Through the miracle of symbols and electricity our own children know everything anyone else knows—the good with the bad. Nothing is mysterious, nothing awesome, nothing is held back from the public view . . . in having access to the previously hidden fruit of adult information, they are expelled from the garden of childhood."
—Neil Postman, The Disappearance of Childhood

Recently, while visiting a large state university, a Christian professor was unable to make his way through the corridors of the Student Union. The crowds were so thick and the students were so intently focused on a TV screen, the visitor supposed some major news story had just broken. Was there another plane crash? A terrorist attack? An earthquake perhaps? The professor waded through the crowd, fully expecting to see Tom Brokaw reporting some international disaster. What he saw was another episode of *Days of Our Lives*.

Far-fetched? Extreme? Not to anyone who knows today's youth. Ours is a media culture; our adolescents literally dwell in an electronic environment. VCRs, CDs, MTV and HBO—these are the acronyms of the information age. The omnipresent media are reshaping the face of American culture—and the church and the home are very much a part of this massive refashioning. Neil Postman, author of *Amusing Ourselves to Death*, argues that television doesn't just reflect our culture. It even goes beyond "shaping" the culture; "television has gradually *become* our culture."[1]

At one time parents could count on rearing their children in a kind of bubble, a spiritually and emotionally secure harbor removed from the world. For a few years at least there was the hope of escaping some of the worst aspects of an adult, fallen world. But that day has long passed. The "staccato signals of constant information" is the nature of the electronic age, so song-writer Paul Simon suggests in "Boy in the Bubble":

> And I believe
> These are the days of lasers in the jungle
> Lasers in the jungle somewhere
> Staccato signals of constant information.

. . .

these are the days of miracle and wonder
This is the long distance call
The way the camera follows us in slo-mo
the way we look to us all

Constantly and in almost all directions, we are at
the mercy of the media, and the media blitz is not a
uniquely American phenomenon. The free flow of
data (both good and bad, sensational or educational)
is unstoppable. It's the price we pay for living in a
postmodern age.

Christian parents are faced with weighty decisions
about how to rear children in a world of hostile, pagan
messages. How does one escape or neutralize the
bewildering onslaught of profane images, the fantastic
mythology of human sexuality that emanates from the
tube, the images of a violently chaotic world seen in
movie after movie? How much can one do about the
frankly erotic, if not pornographic language, of much
popular music? Is it possible for Christian families,
somehow, to escape the "staccato signals of constant
information"?

Some parents are making heroic efforts to control
the quantity and quality of media messages allowed
in their homes. They limit TV watching; a few determined parents even banish the television from the
house altogether. However, the media messages still
descend upon their children just the same—through
radio, cassette players, and CD players blasting lyrics
of shockingly frank language; through massive bill-
boards shouting sex along the freeways; through slick
magazine ads whispering unholy desires; and through
racy movies playing at the local theatres or on home
videocassette players. Postman argues in *Disappearance* that in this culture it is difficult for children

even to experience childhood as we have known it. Exposure to vast stores of "powerful adult material" makes childhood impossible.[2] No one completely escapes, it seems.

Because our children dwell in a pervasive electronic environment, no study of adolescent sexual behavior would be complete without some attention to the role of the media in their lives. Our survey attempted to find out how much the media are impacting our children and how our youths are functioning in a media environment.

Degrees of Media Exposure

We know that most Americans spend large blocks of time watching television; adults spend about five hours a day watching television. Viewing television is the third most important activity, following sleep and work, in terms of time devoted to it.

> The tube is part of our life and our lore. We don't so much watch television as settle into it like a bath, huddle around it like a fire, or treat it as though it were someone else in the room. This goes on for thousands of hours, years even, during a lifetime. It is an awesome force indeed.[3]

One might hope that Christian families would have a different set of priorities when it comes to devotion to television and other media, but our research shows that our kids are media "junkies" as much as the rest. Christian families generally mirror the culture at large.

Television Viewing

- 9% of our adolescents watch five hours or more of television each day
- 24% watch three hours a day
- 24% watch two hours a day
- 16% watch one hour a day
- 7% watch a half hour a day
- 20% seldom or never watch television

Thus, more than half our young people watch television at least two or more hours a day. About a third of our young people view three or more hours of television each day. These figures are comparable to national norms. A.C. Nielsen reports that teens watch about 24 hours of television a week, and children ages 6 through 11 watch 27.5 hours weekly.

Music and Radio

Adolescents also are devoted to listening to music. Many of them are more committed to popular music than to television.

- 25% listen to the radio or musical tapes five hours a day
- 24% listen three to four hours a day
- 24% listen two hours a day
- 15% listen one hour a day
- 8% listen half an hour a day
- 4% seldom or never listen to music

In other words, about three-fourths of our teens listen to two or more hours of music every day. Parents and church leaders surely ought to wonder about the spiritual status of Christian youth who listen to 24 hours of song lyrics each week, but who receive (at best!) one or two hours of religious instruction weekly.

Movies and Videos

- 4% say they watch four or more movies a week
- 13% watch two or three movies a week
- 29% watch at least one a week
- 32% watch one movie every two to three weeks
- 12% watch one movie every four to five weeks
- 10% rarely or never watch a movie

In other words, about half our kids go to a movie or watch a video at least once a week, and more than three-fourths view a movie or video at least every two or three weeks.

We have not attempted to measure the impact of print media (magazines, newspapers, novels, printed advertisements) on our adolescents. Yet when one totals the time controlled just by television, movies and music, one has to be struck by the enormous domination of the electronic media. The big question is, What is this immersion in the electronic world doing to our kids?

What Are They Learning from the Media?

Recognizing that the media are far more than enter-tainment is crucial. They are repositories of distinc-tive values that are presented in powerfully persua-sive ways. Some of these values come through in living color. We find it relatively easy to spot unsa-vory language in a pop song like George Michael's "I Want Your Sex," scenes of nudity in an R-rated film, or the promotion of "non-traditional lifestyles" on a

Phil Donahue show. Perhaps more insidious are the invisible messages that teens and adults often miss.

Furthermore, the unique nature of visual images makes visual messages particularly difficult to resist for most viewers. Printed words call on the mind to think, react and analyze, but movies and television merely ask us to accept as "truth" whatever is seen. What we see with our own eyes, we are predisposed to accept as true. According to Postman, "It cannot be said often enough that, unlike sentences, a picture is irrefutable." The icon, the image, says, "This is truth. This is the way the world is."

Children and teens are especially vulnerable because visual images appeal directly to emotion and feeling, rather than to intellect. Pictures "call upon our emotions, not our reason. They ask us to feel, not to think."[4] This explains why children and adolescents can so easily be moved by and led to imitate what they see on video or film.

We must think carefully about what our children are observing and learning. Like responsible parents concerned with nutrition, we must ask some difficult questions about the heavy diet of popular music, videos, movies and television. The Bible urges believers to receive and meditate on ideas that are noble, right, lovely and admirable (Philippians 4:8). Is this what is happening? What exactly are our adolescents ingesting? We will note some of these negative media messages; some are overt, some hidden.

First, the media teach our teens that people are the sum of their possessions, that happiness comes from acquisitions. Using dreamlike, symbolic pictures to show the path to everlasting happiness, commercials, movies and music videos convey the secular dogma that clothes, decors, furnishings and even locations (Hawaii, New York City, the Caribbean, for example) confer happiness and the good life. These images—powerful, seductive and beautiful—dictate the shape of the American dream, frustrating viewers until they acquire these components of the dream, bit by bit. Quite naturally, the desire for things is fueled by the daily parade of products before one's eyes. Who can resist being a materialist after watching thousands of hours of seductive images year after year?

Second, the media suggest a world of stereotypes. Despite all the claims to "realism" (it's the most common defense advanced by film-makers when consumers complain about language, nudity or violence), three times as many men appear in videos as women. Minorities (including teens and the elderly) are often presented in unflattering terms. Women seldom appear unless they are young and sexually attractive. And sincerely religious characters are almost totally banished.

When you look for the religious aspect to life in Hollywood films and TV shows, the screen goes blank. Where are the devout Christians? Where are the religiously motivated heroes? How often do you see a positive role model going to church? In fact, religion is an "aberrant phenomenon" in contemporary film and television.[5] Consumers of the media get a very strong and consistent message: You can have friends, a job, a family and a rich, full existence, but you can count on it—you will never have to deal with God. The approach to religion is deceit by distortion and omission.

Third, the media present an anti-Christian view of human sexuality. In videoland, promiscuity and permissiveness are perfectly commonplace. Despite the claim that AIDS has ushered in a new era of restraint and "realism," sex outside of marriage is the norm, and extramarital sex has no particular, negative consequences.

The approach to sex in the media is in fact amazingly consistent—sex doesn't happen in marriage. (When it does, it's exceptional.) References to premarital and extramarital sex far surpass references to sex within marriage. The average adolescent, in a year, is exposed through the media to 9,320 sex acts, 81 percent of which are premarital or extramarital. In a 10-year period the average kid sees or hears dialogue referring to more than 93,000 sexual experiences, almost 73,000 of them being outside of marriage. In a typical soap opera, 94 percent of all sexual encounters are extramarital.

A very disturbing development in network television and major motion pictures is the increasing incidence of sexual violence. Many recent box office hits are "cut-and-slash" films that employ sado-masochistic themes, which exploit women. MTV also is known to employ sado-masochistic themes. In fact the explosive succession of violent images is one of the hallmarks of the network. The mix of sex and violence guarantees an audience, but it also portends an increasing number of disturbed persons who will be aroused by what they see. A few will choose to imitate what they see.

The Effects of Media

Quite simply, the media distort reality in several ways. "If you want the truth, don't come to us," says Howard Beale, a character in the movie *Network*. That's a fairly apt summary of the situation. Of course, some consumers of the media have the maturity to separate fantasy from reality, hype from fact. Yet many could not do so even if they wanted to.

All humans are creatures of imitation. Observational learning is an uncontested fact. The accounts of children who meticulously enact what they see are commonplace. All sorts of crimes and antisocial behavior have resulted from children and teens imitating a specific TV show or movie. Countless scientific studies show that children and teens do regularly act out what they watch. The National Institute of Mental Health offers extensive and almost unanimous research proving that this is so.[6]

Just as dozens of carefully controlled studies show a correlation between TV viewing and negative behavior, such as aggression, our survey shows a similar phenomenon. Specifically, sexual attitudes and behavior change when the media dominate adolescents' lives. Steady media consumption means that adolescents are more likely to renounce Christian values and adopt non-Christian ones.

We do not argue that bad programming automatically, or in every case, leads to antisocial or un-Christian behavior. However, when a program with negative content is viewed by millions, one can predict with certainty that large numbers of people (though not all) will be adversely affected. What children see and hear very much affects how they feel, what they think, and what they do. A student wrote a few weeks after Geraldo Rivera's now famous special on the occult:

> I am a 16-year-old who, like many teenagers, spends a lot of time in front of the television. But until I watched Geraldo Rivera's special on Satanism, I didn't realize how greatly television affects a teenager's life. The day after the show, Satanic signs began to appear

on book covers, notebooks and desk tops at my school. Obviously, the show left a bigger impression on kids my age than the producers intended.[7]

What one student observed in his high school has been long known: Children imitate what they see. For network officials to say otherwise is comparable to spokespersons for the tobacco industry saying there's no proven link between smoking and lung cancer. Everyone knows that such a statement is dishonest special pleading. It is axiomatic, then, that the media shape behavior, both positively and negatively, in countless ways.

Our survey of students confirms what others have found, namely, that our youth are being significantly affected by the media. About half our young people claim that sexually explicit materials in the media do affect their thinking and behavior (46 percent). If half the students can admit openly that they are affected by what they see, we may wonder about the other half; how many of them are also affected, but simply unconscious of it?

Adolescent experts like Dr. Sol Gordon and Dr. Herschel Thornberg argue that the primary source of sexual learning is through peer groups, *but the second most important source of sexual instruction is the media;* mother comes third, and father and clergy come in last. The order established by Gordon and Thornberg was, incidentally, confirmed in recent surveys of Christian college students. Because television and movies say and dramatize so much about sex, and because we know that teens consider television and movies as valid sources of "instruction" about sex, we should be scrutinizing the sexual content of television and film.

TV, *Sexual Behavior and Family Values*

In one specific area where one might have expected a statistical correlation (between TV viewing and virginity), we found none. However, high television exposure is linked with pornography usage. Those who watch television five or more hours a day are 14 percent more likely to have been exposed to printed pornography compared to those who are considered low television watchers.

Another effect of television watching is stress on the family's cohesiveness. Television does something to an adolescent's capacity to accept parental values. Teens who watch television excessively are almost twice as likely to reject parental values as adolescents who watch very little television.

Movies and Sexual Behavior

When it comes to movie and video exposure, the picture is bleak. Excessive movie watchers (those who watch four or more per week) are

- Twice as likely to use pornography
- Twice as likely to engage in intimate touching
- Three times more likely to reject parental values

Our survey went beyond measuring the quantity of television and movie viewing; we also determined the amount of "emotional attachment." In almost every category, youths who can be classified as very emotionally attached fare worse than other teens. Teens who could be described as highly attached to movies are:

- Less virginal (73 percent vs. 64 percent)
- Three times more likely to engage in intimate touching
- 33 percent more likely to use pornography

Music and Values

Earlier we reported that radio is a dominant media influence on adolescents. Does listening to music on radio, cassette players, and CD players influence the thinking and actions of our teens? Yes, definitely. Those who listen to music a half hour a day or less have an 81 percent virginity rate, but those who listen five hours or more each day have a 61 percent virginity rate. Apparently, the sexually explicit themes of today's song lyrics, when absorbed by our teens in large doses over time, have a pronounced effect.

A significant correlation also exists between music listening and involvement in intimate touching: 21 percent of those who listen five or more hours a day engage in intimate touching compared to only 10 percent among those who listen two hours a day. Furthermore, excessive listening to music appears to diminish parental influence. The five-hour-a-day listeners are one-third less likely to accept parental influence compared to the one-hour-a-day listeners. Teens who are heavily attached to music are twice as likely to engage in intimate touching, twice as likely to reject parental values, and 25 percent more likely to use pornography.

MTV and Values

Music videos provide an intriguing category. Since its inception, MTV has been noted for its titillating blend of sex and rebellion in flashy, provocative images. Adolescents who are attached to music videos are in several respects likely to mirror the values found in the videos. For example, those attached to MTV are

- 16 percent less virginal (77 percent vs. 61 percent)
- 40 percent more likely to engage in intimate touching
- 40 percent more likely to use pornography
- 35 percent more likely to reject parental values
- 5 times more likely to intend to be sexually permissive on a date

These data support the conclusion that heavy media exposure impacts adolescents negatively. Although moderate exposure is not noticeably damaging (so far as we can tell), strong attachment to the media certainly disturbs the moral development of adolescents.

What our children observe and hear can alter who they are. "None of us are above the laws of learning," certainly not our children.[8] Although our research is preliminary, the evidence we have collected strongly suggests that a deep attachment to the media means a lowering of sexual standards and a loss of identification with parental values. In effect, large doses of the media become a wedge between parents and teens.

Our Response to the Media

Despite all the foregoing, we are not suggesting the media are entirely bad. Television and movies and music provide information, recreation and pleasant forms of escape. On occasion they can even sensitize consciences in remarkable ways. One may recall the autumn of 1984 when millions of Americans were informed by the electronic media of the African famine. Within days after the stark images of suffering appeared on the evening news, Americans had initiated massive relief efforts. The spontaneous outpouring of relief could not have occurred without the compelling images on network broadcasts.

No one disputes the entertaining quality of the media. Movies, music and television provide escape and pleasure in difficult times. A recent university study shows that Christian students who are coping with a divorce in their families turn to television and music as the preferred means of coping with the trauma. Teenagers use music and television as the means to establish their own "space" and identity.

We can appreciate these constructive functions of the media, but what about the bad? What are parents and church leaders to do about the obvious damage that comes from excessive exposure? A number of excellent books and articles are available on the subject. Certain organizations like ACT (Action for Children's Television) and periodicals like *Parents Magazine* offer good advice for controlling the influences of television. However, in summary we suggest that families establish a comprehensive program of "media self-defense" for their families by using the three suggestions listed below.

Above all, *parents must talk with their children about the hidden media messages.* Learning to "talk back" to the tube is one way to resist actively the themes and the ideas o f the media. The goal is to develop children's sophistication in "reading" movies and TV shows. As children mature, parents must make the themes of the media the subject of family discussions. Parents and children should discuss the motivation of characters or the moral problem when evil behavior appears to be approved.

Parents can help children note not only what is included but also what often is excluded (positive values, Christian solutions, realistic consequences, and so forth). When a film glorifies revenge, retaliation, illicit sex, or the rejection of lawful authority, the material can be neutralized partially by discussing objectional material. Parents can override the content of media when they discuss openly and freely what is happening.

As noted before, some of the most dangerous messages are implicit. Materialism, sexism, anti-church biases, and stereotyping are often extremely subtle. How are various classes of people portrayed? How are ministers depicted? How about the fact that genuinely religious types seldom appear? One should discuss the selective omission of settings and themes that don't fit a Hollywood view of life.

Some critics have noted the unusually sanitary world presented by Hollywood, what Lloyd Billingsley calls a "California view of the world," where the "sun shines nearly every day. Cars don't rust or get muddy. Even slums like Watts are positively antiseptic when compared with similar regions in the East."[9] Movies and television often gloss over the world as it is—a broken world in which people experience *spiritual* poverty and desperately long for *spiritual* solutions.

We doubt that children mesmerized by the pulsating images, which change on average every three and a half seconds on network television, can understand the manipulation of the media without extensive guidance and instruction. For this reason, parents and church leaders have an obligation to teach their children to be "media smart," to discern what is being conveyed through image and sound. In summary, we must teach our children to view "world-viewishly."

Second, *we can become more selective about what we watch.* Carefully selected viewing and monitoring is essential. Checking the reviews before we send children off to the theater or the video shop is a minimal parenting responsibility. In a surprising way, the advent of videocassette players and video rental shops actually has increased the opportunities of parental control. More than 50 percent of families decide what to rent on a joint basis. Parents have the opportunity to regain an active role in deciding what their children watch.

The same kind of intelligent supervision can be applied to music listening and other forms of the media. Moderation is a biblical ideal, which is certainly worth applying here.

A third approach is to *limit consumption in a drastic way by engaging in a "media fast."* A media fast is similar to a food fast. In order to withdraw from the domination of the media (whether print or electronic) and in order to focus the mind on spiritual values, one elects to control his exposure to media for a specified period of time. Whole congregations have been called to engage in a media fast for a few days or a week, simply to restore spiritual priorities.

Some families find it excruciating to give up television altogether (perhaps signifying real addiction), but short periods of abstinence can be easily managed. A few days or a single evening may be a good start. This time away from media chatter can be invaluable because it allows families to re-establish personal communication. The television might be interrupting the nurturing that parents would otherwise be providing their children. The television sometimes is nothing less than an electronic surrogate parent, occupying the child but not providing emotional warmth. Time away from the tube allows the restoration of precious ties between parent and child.

Conclusion

The fact is, our children are enveloped by the electronic media. The average teen-ager graduates from high-school having watched 22,000 hours of television. Between the seventh grade and high-school graduation the typical adolescent listens to 10,500 hours of rock music. The day when parents could transfer to their children their most cherished values, without interference or contradiction, passed away in the 1950s as media use blossomed.

Being a Christian parent or a Christian adolescent in such a media-saturated world is extremely difficult, but it is possible. Success, however, requires parents to be vigilant and active, not naive nor passive. Although parents cannot completely control the media affecting their children, they still have some say about the context in which their children receive media messages. They still have the power to converse with their children about family concerns and spiritual values. They can mitigate some media messages.

Furthermore, church leaders and ministers can begin to see their work in a new light. They must consider ways to help families cancel or nullify at least some of the media's hurtful messages. Classes in "media self-defense" are very much in order. What could be more biblical than teaching children the ways and means to resist pagan media messages? After we become conscious of the false messages about human sexuality endlessly emanating from radio, television, movies and magazines, and after we see the damage they are doing to our young, we must resolve to provide healthy new ways to live in a media-saturated culture.

Endnotes

1. Neil Postman, *Amusing Ourselves to Death: Public Discourse in the Age of Show Business* (New York, Viking Press, 1985), 79.
2. Neil Postman, *The Disappearance of Childhood* (New York: Delacorte Press, 1982), 88.
3. Lloyd Billingsley, "TV, Where the Girls Are Good Looking and the Good Guys Win." *Christianity Today* 4 October 1985: 36-41.
4. Postman, *Disappearance of Childhood,* 73.
5. Billingsley, 39.
6. National Institute of Mental Health. *Television and Behavior,* 2 vols. (Washington, D.C.: Government Printing Office, 1982).
7. Anmarie Belknap. Letter. *Newsweek* 12 December 1988: 12.
8. Randy Frame, "Violence for Fun," *Christianity Today* 21 February 1986: 16-17.
9. Billingsley, 36-37.

CHAPTER
9

AFTER THE SILENCE
IS SHATTERED

"Those who do not run away from our pains but touch them with compassion bring healing and new strength. The paradox indeed is that the beginning of healing is in the solidarity with the pain."—Henri Nouwen, Reaching Out

"Speaking the truth in love, we will in all things grow up into him who is the Head, that is, Christ" (Ephesians 4:15).

Throughout this book we have argued implicitly that silence is both good and bad. There is a good kind of silence: the silence that marks fully engaged listening, the silence of the parent concerned to hear the spiritual heartbeat of the child, and of course the silence born of contemplation ("Be still and know that I am God").

But the evil silence is exemplified when a father refuses to talk to his son because he doesn't really want to face the struggles in the boy's life, when a mother refuses to see the signs of desperate loneliness in a daughter's dating behavior, or when a church leader acts as though the sexual problems of teenagers are irrelevant to the congregation's mission. In each of these situations the silence becomes a deadly conspiracy against the truth.

When silence means the refusal to see the truth in our children's lives or when their burning questions and longings for understanding are denied, tragedy is near at hand.

With whom are our children to talk if we deny them an open place for honest dialogue? Where are they to get their answers and their standards? Are they to gain understanding from their confused peers, the latest rock lyrics, or the current film? If we do not listen attentively, generously and non-judgmentally and if we do not speak the truth in love to them, then we certainly are placing stumbling blocks in front of them, which is a perilous act for them and for us. Jesus' harshest words are reserved for adults who place obstacles in the way of youths: "Obstacles indeed there must be, but alas for the man who provides them!" (Matthew 18:7 The Jerusalem Bible).

Christians, above all, love the truth. Paul says it in eloquent simplicity; "Love delights in the truth" (1 Corinthians 13:6 The Jerusalem Bible). And although not all truth is delightful, the truth is necessary. This national survey and study of the youth in churches of Christ is one attempt to shatter the silence.

The truth about our young people's sexual lives is marked by success and disappointment. Most of our young people are making an effort to live godly lives. They do care about and share many of their parents' values. Great numbers of them are serious in their search for God and live on a moral plane above their secular peers. For the most part, they value chastity and traditional family concerns, though their success in achieving a biblical level of morality is uneven. Far too many of them have a naive and legalistic understanding of sexual purity. Great numbers of our young people are being hurt by negative forces and environmental factors which they have only partial control over. Such factors include family life, congregational programs, and the culture at large (including media messages).

This last fact should lead our adult readers to a final point of concern: What is our role in helping children and adolescents survive in the sexual jungle that is modern America? How can we help in this difficult situation? The fact is that parents, youth leaders, ministers and church leaders have significant power over the environmental factors that affect their teens' moral and spiritual lives. Adults cannot completely dictate their children's environment, but our research provides convincing evidence that home life, congregational styles, friendship networks and youth programs, cumulatively, can measurably affect adolescent sexual behavior. Adults have much to say about these factors.

After parents and church leaders realize their efforts can contribute something to their children's moral life, they must choose a wise and reasoned approach. Many well-meaning and otherwise intelligent adults have resorted to unproductive and futile measures, often exacerbating an already difficult situation.

Let us first consider three inadequate or erroneous approaches to helping teens. Then we will look at a "reasoned, Christian approach" that has been proven consistently successful in helping adolescents become responsible, Christian adults.

MISGUIDED APPROACHES

The Parent as Watchdog. Some parents see their role in the family as the all-seeing eye or the ever-vigilant sentry. Some fathers stand at the door like paternal German shepherds on guard against all inter-lopers. The parental watchdog may have virtuous aims, such as protecting the child and the sanctity of the home. But the results may prove meager compared to the damage that comes from living in a prisonlike atmosphere. Often the environment of ex-cessive restraint drives the teen-ager to resist or rebel when a more moderate approach would have met with acceptance and compliance. Homes make very poor convents or monasteries. Keeping the child be-hind walls out of harm's way becomes ever more difficult. The older the child, the higher and thicker must be the walls.

Eventually the watchdog parent loses in one of two ways. First, the pressure usually builds to an intoler-able level, forcing the child to find an escape route, often in a dramatic way (running away, pregnancy, theft and so on). If open resistance is not feasible, the child may find a number of forms of passive rebellion. Nonetheless, whether secretly or openly, the child finds a way out of the box.

Watchdog parents also lose a second way. Even if they succeed in making the home a complete cloister, the child may become so reliant on the parent that he or she remains a child forever, pyschologically dependent, emotionally stunted, and never able to function as an autonomous adult. These parents "succeed" by tragically destroying the potential and full humanity of their offspring.

The strategies of the watchdog parent are numerous. Today this type of parent seldom puts extra locks on the door, but he or she may stand guard in other ways, such as through unreasonably strict rules about dating, curfew and activities. The watchdog attitude may be seen when parents continue to make all the decisions for teen-agers when the children are old enough to make decisions themselves. It may be seen when parents refuse to allow the child to risk anything or fail at anything. Worst of all, the restraints may be enforced through subtle manipulations, such as threats, emotional blackmail and "guilt trips."

Watchdog parents may need as much help as their children to see what they are doing to the children and themselves. They must come to see the futility of their mission. One day, no walls will be high enough. Nearly always the day comes when the locks will be jimmied, the door unbolted, and the child liberated.

The Pretenders. Another dangerous parental type is the pretender, the father or mother who lives in denial. This parent flatly refuses to see his or her children honestly. Pretenders are utterly heedless of the telltale signs of distress in their children's lives. These parents may be highly respected members of the community and pillars of the local church, but they have a monumental blind spot. Perhaps their son carouses on weekends. The daughter may be slipping into promiscuous behavior on dates, and everyone but Mom and Dad know it.

The youth minister sees the scornful look in Jennifer's eyes or in Blaine's not-so-subtle passive aggression at the senior high pizza party. But when the minister talks to the parents about these troubling matters, the parents look at him with vacant wonder. If the parents are polite, they may brush him off with a lame promise to "look into the matter." Sometimes, they are genuinely offended because in their carefully fabricated world view, their children are spotless. They dwell in a fairy-tale world in which the emperor has clothes on because they say he does. It won't do to say otherwise.

The children of such pretending parents occupy a tragically difficult situation. Often the rebellious son or daughter is crying for rescue; however, the louder the child calls for help through his or her misdeeds, the more deaf and blind become the parents. How frustrating it must be for children calling for rescue!

The forms of pretense are various. Pretense may not involve the calculated oversight of negative behavior, but it may come in the form of parents supposing that their children are capable of handling any situation, however tempting. They cannot imagine the difficulties or struggles of their teens, so they allow them excessive freedom. Whatever the circumstance— parties where alcohol flows, a club run by the rough crowd, a fast car, or plenty of spending money—the parents think, "My child can handle it—no problem." The spiritual land mines lie all about, but because they are out of sight, they are out of mind as well. These parents only see the danger when it's too late. Until the explosion, they never imagined that causes have effects, that people reap what they sow.

The Accommodationists. Some parents are aware of their children's circumstances and they may also be aware of the nature of contemporary culture, but they are not particularly alarmed because they believe "Boys will be boys, and girls will be girls." In other words, these "enlightened" parents have no problem accommodating contemporary cultural standards.

The rationalizations come in several packages. "Everyone has to sow his wild oats," some say. Others concede: "I just couldn't do much about it anyway. That's the way things are today."

Whatever one calls it, this approach spells abdication, and it runs counter to biblical Christianity. The Bible presupposes that believers can live in a secular culture without compromising biblical morality. Restraint and moderation are biblical mandates. To suppose that God will simply tolerate or ignore immoral living in any group or individual is "cheap grace." Selling out to the opposition is not a satisfactory solution to the dilemma of being a Christian in a dark world.

However well-meaning, the watchdogs, pretenders and accommodationists are problem parents who actually contribute to their children's troubles. Fortunately, parents can choose a better way to raise children, which we call the reasoned Christian approach.

THE REASONED CHRISTIAN APPROACH

Monica was the mother of one of the world's most famous Christians, but if you had talked to her when her son was an adolescent, she would have told you that having a faithful, devoted Christian son seemed like an impossible dream. Monica reared her son, Augustine, in very difficult circumstances, during the last days of an exhausted, decadent Roman empire, in a culture surprisingly similar to our own.

In his autobiography, *The Confessions*, Augustine recalls a hedonistic culture teeming with every kind of temptation. Theaters specialized in sleazy erotic plays. Sadomasochistic displays could be viewed at the gladiatorial contests. All sorts of new religions mixed elements of Christianity, astrology and Eastern mysticism, very much like today's New Age religions.

The urban centers were particularly noted for corruption. "I came to Carthage," Augustine says, "and all around me in my ears were the sizzling and frying of unholy loves." One could say this description is a rather apt summary of late 20th century culture.

In this setting, Augustine was thirsty for pleasure and fame. He longed to be a man of fashion. At 18 his girlfriend moved in with him, and Monica grieved for her son's soul.

The chances that Augustine would become one of the greatest fathers of the church seemed absolutely remote. Augustine's father was a pagan too, and poor Monica had little help. Monica made a number of mistakes, to be sure. When her son was young and impressionable, he asked to be baptized, but Monica discouraged him, wanting him to wait. When he was willing to marry and avoid fornication, his parents discouraged him, though we don't know their reasons.

Despite her several errors, Monica did many things well. She illustrates many of the best qualities of the "reasoned Christian approach." She was never the watchdog, though she tried to stay close to her son, even when he was disobedient to God. She never "wrote him out of the will" because of his immorality. She was never the pretender or the accommodationist, for she saw Augustine's mistakes with painful clarity, and she prayed for his repentance endlessly.

Once, in anguish, Monica called on one of the elders of the church, a very wise man who had grown up in the faith. He consoled her and confided that he thought the day would come when Augustine would recognize his mistakes and return to the faith. But Monica was unsure and anxious. Above all, she wanted the bishop to argue young Augustine out of his errors. She wept bitterly, asking the spiritual shepherd to do something to convince the boy. But the old man refused, saying, "As you live, it is impossible that the son of these tears should perish." He proved to be correct. Monica's tears and many other experiences were instrumental in leading Augustine to God. The "reasoned approach" can be seen in Monica.

First, wise parents care deeply and passionately for their children and never give up on them. Parents who deeply value their children will pay any price to help them.

Furthermore, they will not let age or experience keep them from identifying with their children's struggles with temptation. They will not treat lightly their son's longing to be included in some peer group. They will not trivialize their daughter's quest for approval and affection. They will recall and understand the pain that attends adolescence. Their children's pains are indeed their own. They can see "that what is most universal is most personal and that indeed nothing human is strange to us." They understand, perhaps intuitively, that "the beginning of healing is in the solidarity with the pain."[1]

The reasoned Christian approach means befriending our children. It means never letting our children become strangers in our own households. Knowing that intimacy is always fading unless someone is actively building bridges, parents who practice the reasoned Christian approach always are looking for opportunities to create an atmosphere of openness and honesty in the household. Topics are freely aired. The truth is told. Differences are respected. Freedom within guidelines is the implicit standard of the house.

And grace is practiced. In the successful Christian household is a wonderful balance of high standards, high expectations, and grace to cover failure. Lewis Smedes is perceptive when he writes in *Sex for Christians:*

> It is, I think, more difficult for adolescents to accept grace than it is for adults. Therefore, it is all the more imperative for Christian parents to mediate God's grace to their children. Children have to taste and feel the grace of God through human grace: the youngster can deeply feel God's acceptance only when if he also feels it through his parents.[2]

In other words, Christian parents find a way to establish rules and standards without losing sight of the fact that being right is a gift of God, not the product of human achievement. Parental love, like God's love, flows constantly, regardless of performance.

Affirmation, encouragement and support often are demonstrated verbally and non-verbally. These parents find it easy to shower affection on their children. Because children need to be noticed, effective parents continue to look at their children, to observe them, and to keep eye contact with them. They know that teens still need touch—a hug, a gentle embrace, and a touch on the shoulder, the back or the arm. Fathers in such families are secure enough in their own sexuality that they can continue to express appropriate physical affection toward their adolescent daughters. Mothers and fathers understand that teen-age sons, not just daughters, need the affirmation and encouragement that come from touch. These parents imitate the divine embrace in loving their children: "I took them up in my arms; I led them with cords of compassion, with bands of love . . . my compassion grows warm and tender" (Hosea 11:3,4,8 The Jerusalem Bible).

Mature parents do not see themselves as the ultimate authority in the family. Rather, they operate within a posture of humility, confessing that Christ is Lord.

Like Monica, their obedience to Christ comes before everything else, and their children observe this commitment. However, church work never becomes a justification for family neglect. Surely Paul is talking about more than food and shelter when he writes: "If anyone does not provide for his relatives, and especially for his immediate family, he has denied the faith and is worse than an unbeliever" (1 Timothy 5:8). When children see fidelity to God and family enacted daily and when they see the integrity of a whole life lived before God under the cross, they are naturally drawn into the circle of faith.

This is not to say that the best efforts of the most discerning parents cannot be thwarted. The heroic efforts of the most committed parents can be cruelly dashed. A prodigal child may wander from the best of homes; however, the return route is much shorter and easier when a warm, embracing parent of integrity stands at one end of the path. This was Monica's situation exactly. When Augustine was ready to return, Monica was anxiously awaiting him.

Isn't that much of the point of Jesus' parable of the lost son in Luke 15? The wise father is the ideal parent, neither watchdog, pretender nor accommodationist. The loving parent continually plants seeds in the child's heart that may bear fruit in the adolescent or in the mature man or woman. No parent should live without hope. Even in his rebellion, the son in the parable panted for his father deep down in the marrow of his soul, and like Augustine, he was restless until he was in his father's arms once again.

The reasoned Christian approach, then, is simply practicing a mature form of charity towards our own children. It is speaking the truth and listening with gentleness. "It is always ready to excuse, to trust, to hope, and to endure whatever comes" (1 Corinthians 13:7 The Jerusalem Bible). Christian parenthood, in short, is being Christ to our children.

A SHARED MINISTRY

From our research and our own experience, we know that helping teen-agers cope with their sexual feelings is difficult at best. Even the most competent parents need all the help they can get. If the church is indeed a body, a community and a family, then the church should provide encouragement and solid resources to struggling families.

Rearing children in earlier cultures was always a shared responsibility. Parents, grandparents, aunts, uncles, ministers and neighbors shared in the duties of bringing up the children of the community. Today, church leaders and ministers must lead the congregation to rediscover the community's responsibility for the community's children.

When the church functions as a family truly concerned for its own, parents will feel less haggard, desperate and besieged. Affluent, technologically advanced cultures have lost much of the sense of community that is desperately needed for successful family life. In *Reaching Out* Henri Nouwen describes the traditional model that we have largely lost:

During a visit to Mexico, sitting on a bench in one of village plazas, I saw how much larger the family of the children was. They were hugged, kissed and carried around by aunts, uncles, friends and neighbors, and it seemed that the whole community spending its evening playfully in the plaza became father and mother for the little ones. Their affection, and their fearless movements made me aware that for them everyone was family.[3]

"Everyone was family." That is the Christian ideal, isn't it? Because our little ones are at stake, wise church leaders do not have time to split hairs over fine points of law. They will sponsor courageous measures to improve congregational life. They will take note of the research in this book that shows "congregational styles" have something to do with the Christian teen's ability to avoid temptation. They will scrutinize the theology flowing from the pulpit and the class lecterns to make sure it is balanced and biblical, adequately conveying the theme of salvation by grace, not works.

Church leaders also will sacrifice and encourage others to sacrifice in order to build the best youth ministry and family life programs possible. This will mean that youth ministry and family ministry will ultimately become one and the same. As the shepherds of a large family, our leaders will rally all God's people to be the mothers and the fathers of all the church's little ones.

Our ministers and leaders will understand and sympathize with the confusion our teens feel as they try to dwell in two competing, vastly different worlds: One is secular, hedonistic and narcissistic, and the other God-centered and self-denying. Christian adults will offer counsel, solace and solutions to teens' very real problems.

Adults think they know what pain and temptation are. They know the anxieties of unpaid bills, lost jobs, broken relationships, and the illnesses and deaths of aging parents. These pains are authentic and anguishing but they are not necessarily any more substantial than those plaguing our teens. Who owns the instrument that measures another person's grief or sorrow?

The struggle for identity and purpose in life, the rejection of peers, the feelings of loneliness, the uncertainty about the future, the bewilderment over rapid physical and emotional changes going on in one's own body—all these things rival our "adult" problems. Adults must especially try to imagine what it is like to grow up in a "sexually supercharged era" in which teens are "bombarded by sexual stimuli as no other generation has."[4] If there is a tie that binds adult heart to adolescent heart, then we will understand and identify with our young in profoundly healing ways. In fact we sing:

> Before our Father's throne
> We pour our arden pray'rs;
> Our fears, our hopes, our aims are one,
> Our comforts and our cares.
> We share our mutual woes,
> Our mutual burdens bear;
> And often for each other flows
> The sympathizing tear.
> "Blest Be the Tie That Binds"—John Fawcett

In many churches, the "youth" of the church are like a dark, silent continent, floating within the fellowship, mostly unknown and essentially misunderstood. "Children are strangers whom we have to get to know," Nouwen remarks.[5] Though strangers in our midst, they are also God's children, known by Him, bearers of the divine image, and the very promise of the church. We must know their story, and we must tell it fearlessly to one another. They have much to teach us, and they have much to learn from us as well.

We can begin by learning where they stand through such surveys as this one. But even better, we can talk with them in a personal, intimate way. We must start with the children in our own dwellings; second, we can communicate with those in our own community of faith and in the larger communities where we reside.

Ultimately, we must *recognize* (i.e., "to re-cognize," "know again" or "remember") what it is like to be a young person. We must "know again" what it is like to be full of life, feeling, doubt, insecurity, longing, idealism, loneliness and passion.

Finally, we must remember that our children do not belong to us. They are temporary gifts on loan to us. Parents share a great deal of responsibility as guardians of these precious God-given gifts, but so does the whole community of faith. If we truly want our children to prosper in the complete sense of the word, that is, to live full, fortunate lives, we must correct and guide them (Ephesians 6:1-4). "Those who have been given a trust must prove faithful," the apostle says (1 Corinthians 4:2).

Today the stewardship of our children means shattering the silence and telling the truth, and telling the truth is part and parcel of a much greater project, namely, to learn how to love our children more fully and adequately. "My little children, love one another." Somehow, we must learn to love our children as Christ loved us. To do less or otherwise, whether we are parents, church leaders, ministers or other church members is to be foolish and unfaithful stewards.

As surely as we expect a gracious Lord to forgive us and save us some day, we must come to know our own children. We must acknowledge their frailties and minister to them. And above all, we must love them so deeply that we feel perfect solidarity with them in their pain, for through this identity healing begins.

We end the silence because silence is a deathly form of denial. Only through speaking the truth in love can we help our children grow up into Him who is the Head, that is Christ.

Endnotes

1. Henri Nouwen, *Reaching Out: The Three Movements of the Spiritual Life* (New York: Doubleday, 1975), 41, 43.
2. Lewis B. Smedes, *Sex for Christians* (Grand Rapids: Eerdmans, 1976), 1964.
3. Nouwen, 58.
4. Smedes, 111.
5. Nouwen, 56.

EPILOGUE:
A FINAL MODEL

One of the most important themes emerging from this research is the holistic nature of all the variables, such as family, ministry, friends and so forth, as they jointly explain sexual behavior. No one variable can be isolated from another if we are to offer any kind of model. Rather, we must recognize that a number of variables work jointly in facilitating moral behavior. The visual model on page 162 demonstrates the results of statistic path analysis, whereby the intercorrelations among a set of predictor variables is teased out into a set of main predictor variables and variables that facilitate the main predictors as they all jointly correlate with virginity.

The major variables are age, church attendance, religious commitment, family system, self-esteem and church system. Of course, age is an obvious developmental factor; when the other main predictors are positive, the likelihood of high virginity rates is high.

Facilitator variables like youth activity attendance, locus of control, attitudes toward church and ministry, family communication, personal faith and church friends are variables that play an essential role as facilitating concepts to the main predictors. These facilitators are not less important qualitatively to the whole system because without them, the whole would not be as powerful as it is. They play a supportive role and are obviously important.

Finally, mass media attachment acts as a detractor variable. That is, mass media takes away from variables such as church attendance, religious commitment and self-esteem. Lack of personal faith, poor family communication and fatalistic locus of control, in fact, link with or contribute to media attachment.

In total, this model accounts for 75% of virginity and 71% of non-virginity. The profile list of significant variables on page 163 also highlights the findings from the study, indicating which elements are of crucial importance.

The chapters already have provided suggestions for various solutions. The point of this model is to adopt a "systems" view. Something special can happen by seeing all these variables as part of a culture—a family culture and a church culture. By visualizing the entire cluster, one is in a better position to diagnose the problem and develop solutions in a holistic fashion.

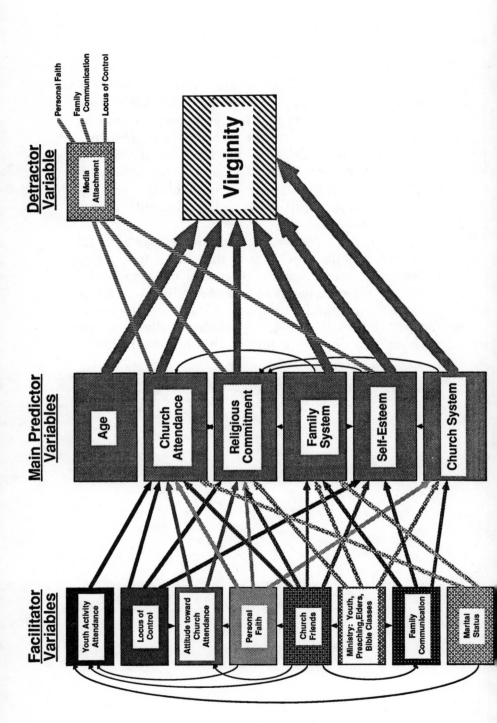

162

PROFILE OF VIRGINS AND NONVIRGINS
TAKEN FROM NATIONAL SURVEY RESULTS

Virgins	Nonvirgins
Younger	Older
Intact families	Divorced families
Supportive family systems	Non-supportive family systems
Positive family communication	Negative family communication
Less identification with non-church friends	Identification with non-church friends
Identify with church friends	Less identification with church friends
Higher self-esteem	Relatively lower self-esteem
Slightly less fatalistic	Slightly higher fatalism
Positive toward youth ministry, preaching, elders and Bible classes	Slightly negative attitude toward youth ministry, preaching, elders and Bible classes
Personal faith higher	Personal faith lower
Come from positive church system	Come from negative church system
Slightly lower movie/video watching and attachment	Slightly higher movie/video watching and attachment
Higher attendance at church and youth activities and positive attendance attitude	Lower attendance at church and youth activities and negative attendance attitude
High religious commitment	Lower religious commitment

These findings explain 75% of virginity.   These findings explain 71% of nonvirginity.

APPENDIX I: METHODS AND INSTRUMENTS

The pilot phase of the study took four months during which survey items were developed from the literature and from personal interviews with clinical and non-clinical adolescents. From that point, a series of 10 pilot versions of the instrument were critiqued by specialists in family therapy, psychology, adolescent development, human relations, school guidance, Bible, human communication, sociology and research design. Furthermore, more than 500 adolescents in churches of Christ took the pilot instrument. A number of these respondents were personally interviewed concerning such issues as honesty, wording and response bias. Their answers indicated suggestions for improved wording, and they demonstrated adolescent comprehension of items on the instrument.

The final instrument resulted in 170 items. The individual scales within the instrument were tested for their internal reliability. The results were a healthy range of Cronback's alpha coefficient of .60 to .92. The more sensitive areas of sexual attitudes and behaviors were cross-checked by asking similar questions throughout the survey. The results revealed high instrument reliability, within the survey's margin of error.

The sample consisted of 2,250 adolescents ranging from 12 to 20 years old. The number yielded a final margin of error of ± 2 percent (at a 95 percent confidence level). The sample was geographically proportionate based on church of Christ populations.

All regions of the United States were represented, however.

Instruments were given to freshmen in five Christian universities for part of the sample and to church of Christ youth throughout the nation who volunteered. Test conditions were controlled for experimenter bias, and complete anonymity was promised and maintained. Questionnaires were sealed by the respondents into envelopes and placed into a box at each test site.

Data were described by frequencies, cross-tabulated using Chi-square, Kendall's Tau and Pearson's r. Cronback's alpha was performed on the scales, and multiple regression, partial correlation and multiple discriminant analysis were used in developing the final path model.

APPENDIX II
SEXUAL ATTITUDES
AND BELIEFS

QUESTIONNAIRE

Let us begin by asking a few questions about you:

1. What is your home state? _____

2. What is your age? (Circle one.)

   12   13   14   15   16   17   18   19   20

3. What is your current grade level in school? (Circle one.)

   7th 8th 9th 10th 11th 12th College   College   College
                                Freshman   Sophomore   Junior

4. What is your sex? (Circle one.) Female   Male
                                      1   2

5. What is your race? (Circle one.)

   Black   Hispanic   Asian   White   Other _____
     1   2   3   4   5

6. Which child in the family order are you? (Circle one.)

   1st   2nd   3rd   4th   Other _____

7. How would you describe your parents' marital status? (Check
   one.)

   _____ 1. My parents have never been separated or divorced.
   _____ 2. My parents have been separated but not divorced.
   _____ 3. My parents have both separated and divorced.
   _____ 4. My parents have divorced and my mother has
             remarried.
   _____ 5. My parents have divorced and my father has remarried.
   _____ 6. My parents have divorced but neither has remarried.
   _____ 7. My parents have divorced and both have remarried.
   _____ 8. None of the above is true of my family. Please explain:

   _____

   _____

   _____

8. If your parents are divorced, how many days on the average do
   you spend with each parent each month?

   1. Father _____   2. Mother _____

9. In my opinion, my family's financial status is (Circle one of the
   numbers below.)

   Extremely wealthy   5   4   3   2   1   Extremely Poor

10. My father's highest educational level is: (Check one.)

_____ 1. Grade school
_____ 2. High school
_____ 3. Some college
_____ 4. College undergraduate degree (B.A., B.S.)
_____ 5. Master's degree
_____ 6. Doctoral degree (Ph.D., M.D., Ed.D., etc.)

11. My mother's highest educational level is (Check one.):

_____ 1. Grade school
_____ 2. High school
_____ 3. Some college
_____ 4. College undergraduate degree (B.A., B.S.)
_____ 5. Master's degree
_____ 6. Doctoral degree (Ph.D., M.D., Ed.D., etc.)

12. How many children are in your family, including brothers, sisters, stepbrothers, stepsisters? _____

13. How would you describe where you live? (Check one.)

_____ 1. Farm or ranch community (up to 1000)
_____ 2. Small town (1000-50,000)
_____ 3. Mid-size city (50,000-200,000)
_____ 4. Large metropolitan area (200,000 and above)

14. What is the size of your home church?

_____ 1. less than 100
_____ 2. 100-200
_____ 3. 200-300
_____ 4. 300-500
_____ 5. 500-800
_____ 6. 800 and above

15. Are you a baptized member of the church?

_____ 1. No
_____ 2. Yes

16. Are your parents members of the Church of Christ?

_____ 1. Neither
_____ 2. Yes, father only
_____ 3. Yes, mother only
_____ 4. Yes, both

Use the scale below to answer each of the following questions concerning your family. Check the number that best shows how you feel about each question.

17. In our family, we are very supportive during tough times.

Almost never   5   4   3   2   1   Almost always

18. Being together is very important to our family.

Almost never   5   4   3   2   1   Almost always

19. I am generally closer to most members of my family than I am to people outside our family.

Almost never   5   4   3   2   1   Almost always

20. When family activities are planned, the whole family usually wants to participate.

Almost never   5   4   3   2   1   Almost always

21. In our family, we discuss important decisions with each other.

Almost never   5   4   3   2   1   Almost always

22. In our family, everyone's suggestions are valued.

Almost never   5   4   3   2   1   Almost always

23. In our family, individual decisions are encouraged.

Almost never   5   4   3   2   1   Almost always

24. In our family, rules are flexible and can change when necessary.

Almost never   5   4   3   2   1   Almost always

25. In our family, we are encouraged to take responsibility for our own actions.

Almost never   5   4   3   2   1   Almost always

When it comes to talking to either or both of my parents about sex:

26. I find it   5   4   3   2   1   I find it
easy to talk   difficult to talk

27. I feel   5   4   3   2   1   I'm scared
very relaxed   to death

28. They seem
to be very
relaxed
___ ___ ___ ___ ___
5   4   3   2   1
They seem
to be
very anxious

29. We can talk
about anything
___ ___ ___ ___ ___
5   4   3   2   1
We can talk about
few things

30. I am very
confident
___ ___ ___ ___ ___
5   4   3   2   1
I become very
embarrassed

31. I speak
and they listen
___ ___ ___ ___ ___
5   4   3   2   1
They speak
and I listen

32. They really
understand
___ ___ ___ ___ ___
5   4   3   2   1
They really don't
understand at all

33. Any time is
a good time
___ ___ ___ ___ ___
5   4   3   2   1
There is never
a good time

34. I feel they
are honest no
matter what
___ ___ ___ ___ ___
5   4   3   2   1
There are times
when I question
their honesty

35. I look
forward
to talking
___ ___ ___ ___ ___
5   4   3   2   1
I would rather
avoid talking

36. I receive
helpful advice
___ ___ ___ ___ ___
5   4   3   2   1
I get no
help at all.

Think for a moment about your friends who are not members of the Church of Christ. Respond below to how you feel about these friends: (Check the number that best fits.)

37. Similar to me
___ ___ ___ ___ ___
5   4   3   2   1
Different from me

38. Smarter
than I am
___ ___ ___ ___ ___
5   4   3   2   1
Less intelligent
than I am

39. They influence
me more than I
influence them
___ ___ ___ ___ ___
5   4   3   2   1
I influence them
more than they
influence me

40. I'm happy
around them
___ ___ ___ ___ ___
5   4   3   2   1
They sadden me

41. They
encourage me
___ ___ ___ ___ ___
5   4   3   2   1
They discourage
me

42. I'm one
of them
___ ___ ___ ___ ___
5   4   3   2   1
I feel
left out

43. Very
religious
___ ___ ___ ___ ___
5   4   3   2   1
Not at all
religious

Now think about your friends who are members of the Church of Christ. Respond below to how you feel about these friends. (Check the number that best fits.)

44. Similar to me   __ __ __ __ __   Different from me
                    5 4 3 2 1

45. Smarter than   __ __ __ __ __   Less intelligent
    I am   5 4 3 2 1   than I am

46. They influence   I influence them
    me more than I   __ __ __ __ __   more than they
    influence them   5 4 3 2 1   influence me

47. I'm happy   __ __ __ __ __   They sadden me
    around them   5 4 3 2 1

48. They   __ __ __ __ __   They
    encourage me   5 4 3 2 1   discourage me

49. I'm one   __ __ __ __ __   I feel
    of them   5 4 3 2 1   left out

50. Very   __ __ __ __ __   Not at all
    religious   5 4 3 2 1   religious

Most of my close friends come from which of the following groups? (Check one of the groups below.)

_____ 51. Church of Christ (your home church)
_____ 52. Church of Christ (places other than your home congregation)
_____ 53. Other religious group. Specify: _____
_____ 54. Non-religious

For each question below, check the number (from 1-5) that tells how you feel about yourself.

55. I often   __ __ __ __ __   I rarely feel
    feel useless   5 4 3 2 1   useless

56. I am   I am
    basically   __ __ __ __ __   basically
    unhappy   5 4 3 2 1   happy

57. I often   __ __ __ __ __   I seldom
    feel inferior   5 4 3 2 1   feel inferior

58. I do few   __ __ __ __ __   I do many
    things well   5 4 3 2 1   things well

59. I am   __ __ __ __ __   I am seldom
    often afraid   5 4 3 2 1   afraid

60. I have little to be proud of   __ __ __ __ __   I have much to be proud of
       5   4   3   2   1

61. I wish I were someone else   __ __ __ __ __   I am glad I am myself
       5   4   3   2   1

62. I often get discouraged   __ __ __ __ __   I seldom get discouraged
       5   4   3   2   1

Beside the following statements, indicate your level of agreement or disagreement by showing whether or not you strongly agree (SA), agree (A), feel neutral (N), disagree (D), or strongly disagree (SD). (Circle your answer for each question.)

63. Luck plays a major role in my life.

     SA   A   N   D   SD
     5   4   3   2   1

64. In the long run, both the bad and the good things that happen to me are beyond my control; what will happen will happen.

     SA   A   N   D   SD
     5   4   3   2   1

65. Many times I am a victim of circumstances that are beyond my control.

     SA   A   N   D   SD
     5   4   3   2   1

66. Most of the time I feel that I have enough control over the direction my life is taking.

     SA   A   N   D   SD
     5   4   3   2   1

67. No matter what they do, some people seem born to fail while others seem born to succeed.

     SA   A   N   D   SD
     5   4   3   2   1

68. I can usually determine and direct my own destiny.

     SA   A   N   D   SD
     5   4   3   2   1

69. No matter how hard you try some people just don't like you.

     SA   A   N   D   SD
     5   4   3   2   1

Some young people have found their local church to be very helpful, while other young people have found little help in dealing with sexual struggles. How would you evaluate the following? (Circle your answer for each question.)

70. Youth ministry of your church:

4	3	2	1
Very Helpful	Somewhat Helpful	Occasionally Helpful	Not at all Helpful

71. Preaching at your church:

4	3	2	1
Very Helpful	Somewhat Helpful	Occasionally Helpful	Not at all Helpful

72. Bible classes at your church:

4	3	2	1
Very Helpful	Somewhat Helpful	Occasionally Helpful	Not at all Helpful

73. Elders at your church:

4	3	2	1
Very Helpful	Somewhat Helpful	Occasionally Helpful	Not at all Helpful

74. Personal faith in God:

4	3	2	1
Very Helpful	Somewhat Helpful	Occasionally Helpful	Not at all Helpful

How would you personally evaluate your home church on the following criteria? (Check the number that best shows how you feel.)

75. Overly strict   5 4 3 2 1   Permissive

76. Legalistic   5 4 3 2 1   Grace-oriented

77. Holds grudges   5 4 3 2 1   Forgiving

78. Out of touch   5 4 3 2 1   Relevant

79. Insensitive   5 4 3 2 1   Sensitive

A series of items appears below that asks for your response concerning various media sources. Tell how much you are exposed to that media source:

80. On the average, my TV watching every day comes out to about: (Check the number that best shows how you feel about this question.)

_____ 7. 5 hours/day
_____ 6. 3-4 hours/day
_____ 5. 2 hours/day
_____ 4. 1 hour/day
_____ 3. ½ hour/day
_____ 2. I seldom watch TV
_____ 1. I never watch TV

81. List your 3 favorite TV shows:

1. _____
2. _____
3. _____

82. On the average, my radio and/or music listening each day comes out to about: (Check the one that best shows how you feel about this question.)

_____ 7. 5 hours/day
_____ 6. 3-4 hours/day
_____ 5. 2 hours/day
_____ 4. 1 hour/day
_____ 3. ½ hour/day
_____ 2. I seldom listen to radio or music
_____ 1. I never listen to radio or music

83. List your 3 favorite music groups

1. _____
2. _____
3. _____

84. On the average, how often do you go to the movies or watch a video? (Check one.)

_____ 7. 4 or more per week
_____ 6. 2-3 per week
_____ 5. 1 per week
_____ 4. Once every 2 or 3 weeks
_____ 3. Once every 4 or 5 weeks
_____ 2. I seldom go to a movie or watch videos
_____ 1. I never go to a movie or watch videos

85. List your 3 favorite movies within the past year:

1. _____
2. _____
3. _____

Some people have very strong attachments to media sources, while others are hardly attached at all. How would you rate your attachment to the following? (Check the number that best shows how you feel.)

86. TV

| Major part of my life | __ 5 | __ 4 | __ 3 | __ 2 | __ 1 | Not all that important to me |

87. RADIO

| Major part of my life | __ 5 | __ 4 | __ 3 | __ 2 | __ 1 | Not all that important to me |

88. MOVIES

| Major part of my life | __ __ __ __ __ | Not all that |
| | 5 4 3 2 1 | important to me |

89. MUSIC VIDEOS

| Major part of my life | __ __ __ __ __ | Not all that |
| | 5 4 3 2 1 | important to me |

Now tell us about your personal religious life: (Check the number that best shows how you feel.)

90. How frequently do you attend services at your church?

_____ 6. rarely
_____ 5. once a month
_____ 4. 2 to 3 times a month
_____ 3. once a week
_____ 2. twice a week
_____ 1. three or more times a week

91. When there is a church youth activity, how often do you attend?

_____ 5. all the time
_____ 4. most of the time
_____ 3. some of the time
_____ 2. rarely
_____ 1. never

92. Some young people attend services at church not by their personal choice, but because of pressure from others to attend, while other young people actually enjoy attending services. Where would you say you fit on the scale below?

| Prefer not to be there | __ __ __ __ __ | Really do want to be there |
| | 5 4 3 2 1 | |

93. Some young people see themselves as having a very personal religious commitment, while other young people do not see themselves that way. How would you evaluate yourself on a religious/non-religious scale?

| Feel little or no personal religious commitment | __ __ __ __ __ | Feel high personal religious commitment |
| | 5 4 3 2 1 | |

There are many teenagers who have decided not to become sexually active with members of the opposite sex. In your opinion, how would you rate the following reasons why teenagers have made this decision? (Circle 1, 2, or 3 beside each item below.)

	Very Important Reason	Somewhat Important Reason	Of Little Importance As a Reason
ITEMS			
94. Fear of AIDS	3	2	1
95. Fear of pregnancy	3	2	1
96. Wish to wait till marriage	3	2	1
97. No real desire or interest	3	2	1
98. Parental disapproval	3	2	1
99. Afraid of unknown	3	2	1
100. Peer disapproval	3	2	1
101. Because God said no	3	2	1
102. They would feel guilty	3	2	1
103. No opportunity	3	2	1
104. Afraid of being hurt	3	2	1
105. Past trauma or bad sexual experience	3	2	1
106. Other _____	3	2	1

There are many teenagers who have decided to become sexually involved with a member(s) of the opposite sex before they are married. Of these teenagers who are sexually involved, how would you rate the following reasons for their involvement? (Circle 1, 2, or 3 beside each item below.)

	Very Important Reason	Somewhat Important Reason	Of Little Importance As a Reason
ITEMS			
107. Pressure by boy/girl friend	3	2	1
108. Pressure of being laughed at, ridiculed, or rejected for remaining a virgin.	3	2	1
109. Rebellion toward parents	3	2	1
110. To be loved	3	2	1

111. Low self-esteem	3	2	1
112. Prove manhood/ womanhood	3	2	1
113. Think they are in love	3	2	1
114. Alcohol or drug abuse	3	2	1
115. Pleasurable	3	2	1
116. Didn't think about consequences	3	2	1
117. Swept away	3	2	1
118. Too much unsupervised time with boyfriend/ girlfriend	3	2	1
119. Other _____	3	2	1

Teenagers have different opinions as to what is right and wrong when it comes to dating. In your opinion, what is acceptable at each of the following stages? (Circle the number to the right of each dating stage.)

Dating Stage   Circle the code number.

120. First date   1 2 3 4 5 6 7 8
                                        Answer code

121. 2-4 dates   1 2 3 4 5 6 7 8   1. sitting close to each other

122. Dating between   1 2 3 4 5 6 7 8   2. holding hands
     2 and 4 months   3. kissing
                                          4. deep kissing on lips

123. Steady dating   1 2 3 4 5 6 7 8   5. intimate touching above waist

124. Steady with   1 2 3 4 5 6 7 8   6. intimate touching below the waist
     discussion of
     possible
     engagement
                                          7. oral sex
                                          8. intercourse

125. Engaged   1 2 3 4 5 6 7 8

126. How would you label the current sexual attitudes among teenagers within Churches of Christ? (Check the number that best shows how you feel.)

Very permissive   5   4   3   2   1   Very conservative

In your opinion, what percentages of all teenagers fall in the three categories below when it comes to their sexual practices?

127. _____ Still virgins
128. _____ Having intercourse, but only in committed relationships
129. _____ Having intercourse, without committed relationships

In your opinion, what percentages of teenagers who are members of the Church of Christ fall into the three categories below when it comes to their sexual practices?

130. _____ Still virgins
131. _____ Having intercourse, but only in committed relationships
132. _____ Having intercourse, without committed relationships

133. What is your opinion about the "sinfulness" of homosexuality? (Circle the number that best shows how you feel.)

4	3	2	1
Definitely sinful	It depends on the circumstances	Haven't decided	Not a sin

134. In your judgment, what should our response be to those who are homosexuals and are members of the Church of Christ? (Circle the number that best shows you you feel.)

4	3	2	1
Basically exclude this person	Accept if they are sorry and change	Accept if they are sorry but continue homosexuality	Accept them no matter what

135. How would you evaluate your parents' influence upon your sexual beliefs and behaviors? (Circle one.)

4	3	2	1
Very Influential	Somewhat Influential	Occasionally Influential	Not at all Influential

136. Are your present values and beliefs similar or different from your parents'? (Check the number along the line that best represents your feelings.)

I am almost identical to my parents' beliefs ___ ___ ___ ___ ___ I am miles apart from my parents' beliefs
5 4 3 2 1

137. How would you evaluate the influence of Christian books and magazines upon your sexual beliefs and behaviors? (Circle one.)

Extremely helpful ___ ___ ___ ___ ___ Not at all helpful
5 4 3 2 1

138. In your opinion, which of the statements below best represents your view about abortion? (Check one statement.)

     5. An important and useful means of population control.

     4. A convenience to be used if necessary.

     3. A reasonable solution when a girl gets pregnant and marriage is not realistic.

     2. Morally questionable, but occasionally justified in cases of rape, certainty of a deformed child, danger to mother's life, etc.

     1. Murder and never justifiable.

139. What is your opinion about masturbation? (Check the number that best shows how you feel.)

Normal part of growing up, nothing wrong with it					Abnormal, sinful and disgusting
5	4	3	2	1	

140. When it comes to your own sexual beliefs, how would you rate yourself on the following scale? (Check the number that best shows how you feel.)

I have a strong need to conform to my peers					I can resist peer pressure easily
5	4	3	2	1	

141. Do you feel that it is very important that your prospective mate be a virgin when you marry? (Circle the number that best shows how you feel.)

4	3	2	1
Extremely important	Very important	Somewhat important	Of little importance

142. In your opinion, what is the impact of sexually suggestive media, such as love scenes on soap operas, sexually suggestive lyrics in songs, etc., upon teenagers' sexual values and behaviors? (Check the number that best shows how you feel.)

Absolutely of no consequence					Major influence in their lives
5	4	3	2	1	

143. What is your opinion about the future of someone who has already decided to become sexually involved with a member of the opposite sex? (Check the number that best shows how you feel.)

Past is forgiveable, so future looks promising					Past is unforgiveable, so why even try Christian sexual standards?
5	4	3	2	1	

144. In your opinion, what is the best advice one could give an anxious parent, who is overly worried about his/her teenager's sexual behavior?

_____

_____

_____

145. In your opinion, what should a parent not do or say to their teenager about teenage sexuality?

_____

_____

_____

146. What was the best piece of advice that you have received so far when it comes to dealing with your own sexuality?

_____

_____

_____

147. To what extent would you define your own sexual behaviors as being consistent with the Bible? (Check the number that best shows how you feel.)

_____ 1. I frankly make no attempt to be consistent
_____ 2. I am usually inconsistent
_____ 3. I try at times to be consistent, and usually am
_____ 4. I am completely consistent

148. Which of the statements below most accurately describes your own involvement in the act of masturbation? (Check the number that best shows how you feel.)

_____ 1. I have never masturbated at all
_____ 2. I never masturbate more than once every few months
_____ 3. I masturbate at least once a month
_____ 4. I masturbate at least once a week
_____ 5. I masturbate 3-5 times a week, or even more
_____ 6. I masturbate once a day

149. On the scale below please indicate how far you have ever gone sexually with a member of the opposite sex. (Circle one.)

1	2	3	4	5	6	7
Holding Hands	Kissing on lips	Deep Kissing	Intimate Touching Above the Waist	Intimate Touching Below the Waist	Oral Sex	Sexual Intercourse

150. If you have had sexual intercourse, how many different sexual partners would you say you have had up to this point? (Check the number that best shows how you feel.)

_____ 4. 8+
_____ 5. 6-7
_____ 6. 4-5
_____ 7. 2-3
_____ 8. One
_____ 9. This question doesn't apply to me

151. If you have had sexual intercourse, what was the age of your first sexual experience? (Check one.)

_____ 1. 13 or younger
_____ 2. 14
_____ 3. 15
_____ 4. 16
_____ 5. 17
_____ 6. 18 or older
_____ 7. This question doesn't apply to me

152. If you have had sexual intercourse, with whom was your first premarital sexual intercourse? (Check one.)

_____ 1. Fiance
_____ 2. Steady
_____ 3. My date; he/she wanted to, but I didn't want to
_____ 4. Casual date, we intended to
_____ 5. Casual date that went too far
_____ 6. Older person that took advantage of me
_____ 7. Family member
_____ 8. This question doesn't apply to me

153. If you have had sexual intercourse, have you ever become pregnant? (Check one.)

_____ 1. Yes, I have had intercourse and I think I'm pregnant.
_____ 2. Yes, I have had intercourse and I know I'm pregnant.
_____ 3. Yes, and the baby was adopted.
_____ 4. Yes, and I kept the baby.
_____ 5. Yes, and I had an abortion.
_____ 6. No, I've not become pregnant.
_____ 7. This question doesn't apply to me, since I've never had intercourse.

154. If you have become sexually active, what form of birth control have you typically used in your premarital intercourse incidents? (Check one.)

_____ 1. The pill
_____ 2. Diaphragm
_____ 3. Condoms (rubbers)
_____ 4. Foam, jelly or cream
_____ 5. Withdrawal
_____ 6. I use no form of birth control
_____ 7. This question doesn't apply to me

155. To what extent have you, and your boy/girl friend(s) engaged in intimate touching to satisfy sexual desires, as a way to maintain your virginity without actually having intercourse? (Check one.)

Almost all the time in serious relationships						Have never engaged in this with a member of the opposite sex
	5	4	3	2	1	

156. In your opinion, which are the following sexual conditions that best currently describe you? (Check one.)

_____ 1. A virgin
_____ 2. Sexual intercourse in the past, but intend to abstain from intercourse until marriage
_____ 3. Sexual intercourse, but only in a committed relationship
_____ 4. Sexual intercourse, but no need for committed relationship

157. At what age did you first begin dating? (Check one.)

_____ 1. 13 or below
_____ 2. 14
_____ 3. 15
_____ 4. 16
_____ 5. 17
_____ 6. 18
_____ 7. I've not begun dating, so this doesn't apply to me.

158. Have you ever experienced any of the following behaviors by a member of your family, either by choice or by force, such as playful touching, deep kissing, intimate touching or sexual intercourse? (Check one or more.)

_____ 1. No
_____ 2. Yes, by my father
_____ 3. Yes, by my stepfather
_____ 4. Yes, by my mother
_____ 5. Yes, by my stepmother
_____ 6. Yes, other—Please specify _____

159. If you answered yes to question 158 by checking 2 through 6 above, then circle to what extent:

1	2	3	4
Playful but inappropriate touching	Romantic deep kissing	Intimate touching fondling	Sexual intercourse

160. Have you personally ever contracted a Sexually Transmitted Disease? (Check one.)

_____ 1. No
_____ 2. Yes

If yes, which?

_____ 3. Syphilis
_____ 4. Gonorrhea
_____ 5. Genital Herpes
_____ 6. AIDS
_____ 7. Other _____

161. Do you know anyone, for a fact, who has AIDS or some other Sexually Transmitted Disease? (Check one.)

_____ 1. Yes, 6 or more
_____ 2. Yes, several, 4 or 5
_____ 3. Yes, 2 or 3
_____ 4. Yes, one
_____ 5. I don't know anyone.

162. Do you personally know anyone who professes to be an active homosexual? (Check one.)

_____ 1. Yes, 6 or more
_____ 2. Yes, several, 4 or 5
_____ 3. Yes, 2 or 3
_____ 4. Yes, one
_____ 5. I don't know anyone.

163. Have you ever used drugs or alcohol in order to enhance a sexual experience? (Check one.)

_____ 1. This question doesn't apply to me.
_____ 2. No, I've never used drugs or alcohol in this way.
_____ 3. Yes, I have used drugs or alcohol in this way.

      If yes, indicate any or all types used:

           _____ 164. Alcohol
           _____ 165. Ecstasy
           _____ 166. Marijuana
           _____ 167. Cocaine
           _____ 168. Other _____

169. When you go out on a date, which of the following best describes your intentions when it comes to sexual behaviors? (Check one.)

_____ 1. Intend to have little or no physical touching.
_____ 2. Intend to engage in light touching, nothing more.
_____ 3. Intend to engage in kissing and embracing.
_____ 4. Intend to engage in intimate touching and fondling.
_____ 5. Intend to engage in sexual intercourse if the condition is right.
_____ 6. Intend to engage in sexual intercourse unless my date doesn't want to.

170. How frequently do you look at sexually explicit materials (such as *Playboy, Playgirl,* X-rated videos, etc.): (Check one.)

_____ 5. At least once a week
_____ 4. Frequently, 2-3 times a month
_____ 3. Occasionally, about every month or two
_____ 2. Rarely, once or twice a year
_____ 1. Never

Thank you for your help in this very important area of teenage Christian development.